ATTENTION — WARNING TO THE READER:
Special Considerations for Nicoderm® (nicotine transdermal system) Use

This book provides helpful information which can assist you in your attempt to stop smoking. This book is provided as a useful aid to a comprehensive behavioral modification program.

NICODERM and Nicorette® (nicotine polacrilex) are indicated as an aid to smoking cessation for the relief of nicotine withdrawal symptoms. Nicoderm or Nicorette should be used as part of a comprehensive behavioral smoking-cessation program. The use of NICODERM for longer than 3 months has not been studied. Nicorette should not be used for longer than 6 months. You should stop smoking completely before using these products and not use any other nicotine containing products during treatment.

Because these products, like cigarettes, could harm your baby, if you are pregnant or nursing you should discuss other ways to stop smoking with your doctor.

Because these products, like cigarettes, contain nicotine, if you have cardiovascular disease you should discuss other ways to stop smoking with your doctor.

There may be other risks associated with the use of these products. If you are taking other medications or are under a doctor's care for another condition, you should discuss this with your doctor.

See Patient Instructions at back of book.

How Heavy Smokers Can Become Nonsmokers

using a comprehensive behavioral smoking-cessation program with Nicoderm®
(nicotine transdermal system)

The Cooper/Clayton Method

by
Thomas M. Cooper, D.D.S.
and
Richard R. Clayton, Ph.D.

Copyright 1993
U.S. Patent Number: 5,055,478
Method for Stopping Smoking
Issued 8 October 1991

Thomas M. Cooper and Richard R. Clayton
Lexington, Kentucky

Library of Congress Cataloging in Publication Data

Main Entry under title

How Heavy Smokers Can Become Nonsmokers Using A
Comprehensive Behavioral Smoking-Cessation Program With
Nicoderm® (nicotine transdermal system): The Cooper/Clayton
Method

Bibliography:

1. Smoking Cessation
2. Nicotine Replacement Therapy
3. Heavy Smokers
4. Nicotine Fading
5. Nicotine Addiction

1 DNLM

1. Fear — smoking
2. Patients — nicotine addiction
3. Medication — alternate nicotine sources
4. Cessation — heavy smokers

Library of Congress Catalog Card Number:
ISBN # 0-962-1398-1-5

Published by: Printed by:
SBC/SBC Inc.   Lee Corp.
826 Glendover   12055 Mosteller Road
Lexington, KY 40502   Cincinnati, OH 45241

Printed in the United States of America

FROM THE AUTHORS

Writing and publishing a book are done with the help of many people. We want to acknowledge the contribution of a few who were especially helpful to us. Our thanks and appreciation go to:

The hundreds of patients who shared their feelings and experiences with us as we met with them in support groups designed to help them become and remain nonsmokers.

Our families who supported our efforts as we worked many evenings, when we otherwise would have been with them; to Bill, Amy, Polly, David, and Tommy, and to Charlyn, Brent, Reid, and Shannon, we love you and are proud of you.

To Lois and Nancy, our spouses and our best friends, thanks for sharing our lives.

PLEASE READ BEFORE YOU CONTINUE.......

Dear Reader:

It is probably safe to guess you picked up this book because of your interest in cigarette smoking cessation. You may be a smoker who feels it is time to become a nonsmoker. Possibly, someone dear to you needs the information. Perhaps you are only curious about what the Cooper/Clayton Method to Stop Smoking is all about.

Regardless of your reason, this book, as part of a comprehensive behavioral smoking-cessation program, can be of value to you. If you smoke, and need to stop, we think it may be the answer you have been searching for. If that special person needs this book, give it as a gift. If you are only curious, we will tell you what the Cooper/ Clayton Method is.

1. The method was developed by a heavy smoker to get him off cigarettes, and has been refined with the aid of an expert on drug addiction.

2. The method assumes that nicotine is an addicting drug.

3. It is especially helpful for heavy smokers who have failed in attempts to become nonsmokers.

4. It is a method used by hundreds of heavy smokers to win their battles against dependence on cigarettes.

5. It is a method that not only helps people get off cigarettes, but helps them to stay off cigarettes.

6. The Cooper/Clayton Method has a very high success rate. Documented evidence in one study of success rates among several hundred smokers who used the Cooper/Clayton Method indicates that approximately 40-45% (49/108) of ALL who began the program are still ex-smokers at the one year point.

7. It makes sense. It first alters the way the smoker supplies nicotine to the brain, then slowly and gently reduces the alternate nicotine source to zero.

8. It has not only helped hundreds to stop smoking, it has taught them to live as adults without nicotine. Yes, Virginia, or Virgil, or Vernon, or Vera, THERE IS A LIFE AFTER NICOTINE!

9. It makes the transition from smoker to ex-smoker manageable; not pain-free, but manageable.

10. The behavioral program is built around the assumption that you taught yourself to smoke. Your brain receptor sites began to expect nicotine daily. The Cooper/Clayton Method for Smoking Cessation works because what you taught yourself can be reversed, un-teach yourself, and ONLY YOU can do it.

11. The Cooper/Clayton Method is NOT a magic cure. It requires significant effort on the part of the smoker, but can be easier when compared to attempting to go COLD TURKEY.

12. The information in this book will or can guide you through your journey from smoker to ex-smoker. Giving up smoking, however, requires a significant change for most people. Typically, when a group of people work together to resolve a common problem, and share experiences of making changes in their lives, chances for success increase significantly. This book can answer many questions you may have. We encourage you to seek out a group smoking-cessation program near you to enjoy the additional benefits of group interaction.

Whether you are the smoker, or someone concerned about a smoker, recognize this fact:

Many of the folks who can lay down their cigarettes, and walk away with minimal discomfort, have already quit. Those who are left include many HEAVY SMOKERS — those who can benefit from a program such as this to win their battle with cigarettes. This book contains a plan — a structured program to assist the smoker to first achieve victory over dependence on cigarettes, and then victory over dependence on nicotine. If that sounds interesting, read on. Hundreds have profited because they did.

****

PLEASE NOTE:

We strongly urge you to examine Figure 2.1 in Chapter 2 prior to reading the rest of this book. That illustration provides an overview of the total 24 weeks of the Cooper/Clayton Method and will probably make the narrative descriptions in Chapters 2 through 8 easier to understand.

****

The information provided in this book has primarily come from two sources. The first is our clinical experience with several hundred heavy smokers who joined a support group using the Cooper/Clayton Method. They have taught us well. The second source is medical literature. Among those who have conducted highly significant research in many forms of chemical dependence is Dr. Jack Henningfield of the Addiction Research Center in Baltimore, Maryland. We are pleased to note that Dr. Henningfield's research on nicotine dependence led him to many of the same conclusions that we reached in a clinical setting.

From May of 1984 until January of 1992, our work with smokers consisted of the use of Nicorette® (nicotine polacrilex) gum as an aid to a comprehensive behavioral smoking-cessation program. Since January of 1992, we have been using nicotine transdermal patch therapy predominantly. The program described in this book will use a prescription product called Nicoderm® (nicotine transdermal system), an aid to smoking cessation for the relief of nicotine withdrawal symptoms. Nicoderm treatment should be used as part of a comprehensive behavioral smoking-cessation program.

Henningfield and Nemeth-Coslett state the following about the length of time over which smoking cessation efforts should take place.

> ...nicotine treatment can reduce anxiety, stress and irritability which are prominent symptoms in tobacco withdrawal and frequent situations in which relapse to tobacco abuse occurs. Taken together, the finding that abstinence effects may persist for months and even years, environmental stimuli can elicit effects associated with drug taking, and relapse actually occurs in expected situations if such protracted abstinence and conditioning occurred with tobacco suggest that TREATMENT APPROACHES FOR TOBACCO DEPENDENCE MUST BE LONG TERM WITH A FOCUS ON MAINTENANCE OF ABSTINENCE AND AVOIDANCE OF RELAPSE (our emphasis).

The Cooper/Clayton Method consists of 24 weeks of behavioral training—two weeks to determine smoking patterns and 22 weeks to learn to live without cigarettes (relapse prevention). The medication period, during which time the patient will receive Nicoderm typically lasts 10-16 weeks as determined by your physician or dentist who prescribes the medication. The remaining portion of the 24 weeks continues the comprehensive behavioral smoking-cessation program and continued relapse prevention. You should note that, to this date, use of Nicoderm beyond 12 weeks has not been studied.

Finally, the same researchers state that:

Now that tobacco use has been more universally accepted as a form of drug dependence in which nicotine is the critical abuse-producing agent, there is a rational basis for the treatment of cigarette smoking based on experience with other forms of drug dependence. While such a conclusion will discourage some, for most it should come as a relief to discover that their difficulties in quitting and the pleasures they associate with tobacco are not merely psychological, they are also physically based. Moreover, they can be treated. IN FACT, THE ACKNOWLEDGMENT AND ACCEPTANCE OF NICOTINE DEPENDENCE IS ACTUALLY REASON FOR ENCOURAGEMENT IN TREATING CIGARETTE SMOKING, FOR IT PROVIDES A RATIONAL BASIS FOR COMBINING PHARMACOLOGIC INTERVENTION WITH BEHAVIORAL TECHNIQUES (our emphasis).

The Cooper/Clayton Method treats nicotine as an addicting substance and lasts a total of 24 weeks. We are convinced there are no quick fixes in smoking cessation. You cannot change overnight all the behavior that has been associated with smoking for 25, 30, or 40 years. Anyone in our program who claims to be a nonsmoker at 1 year, 2 years, 3 years, 5 years is asked to provide verification of nonsmoking status by an exhaled air carbon monoxide reading. Everyone who comes into the program and receives a prescription for nicotine replacement therapy is put into our denominator. Even if they never come to any more meetings and we can't find them to even ask if they are nonsmokers, they go into our denominator.

Our published success rates using the nicotine gum can be found in the January 1989 and January 1990 issues of the Journal of the American Dental Association. The first article reports the 1 year followup success rates for 118 heavy smokers; 40% were verified as nonsmokers. The second article reports the 1 year and 3 year success rates for 108 patients who used the Cooper/Clayton Method. The 1 year success rate was 49/108 or 45% chemically verified as nonsmokers. Of these, 36% or 39/108 were still nonsmokers at 3 years beyond beginning the Cooper/Clayton Method. These were re-interviewed at 5 years beyond entering the Cooper/Clayton program; only one had relapsed between year 3 and year 5. Sadly, 2 of the nonsmokers had died. Removing them from the data still resulted in a 5 year success rate of 34%. Therefore, the 5 year success rate for these heavy smokers was 34% chemically verified. An article describing the 5 year followup data is now in preparation.

Our 24 week success rates using the nicotine transdermal patch system is slightly in excess of 50%, which is comparable to the results we achieved with the nicotine gum (Thomas M. Cooper and Richard R. Clayton, Nicotine Transdermal Patches: The Efficacy, Safety, and Effect on Withdrawal Symptoms, submitted for publication, October 1992).

The truth is — not everyone is successful. Becoming a nonsmoker and breaking your dependence on nicotine may be the hardest thing you will ever try to accomplish. If you are successful, and we know you can be successful, there is virtually nothing you cannot achieve if you try.

WE WISH YOU SUCCESS!

Thomas M. Cooper   **Richard R. Clayton**

CHAPTER 1

DEVELOPMENT OF THE COOPER/CLAYTON METHOD TO BECOME A NONSMOKER

"To hope is to risk pain. And, to try is to risk failure. But risk must be taken, because the greatest hazard in life is to risk NOTHING. The person who risks nothing does nothing, has nothing, and is nothing. He may avoid suffering and sorrow, but he simply cannot learn, feel, change, grow, live, or love. Chained by his certitudes or his addictions, he's a slave. He has forfeited his greatest trait, and that is his individual freedom. Only the person who risks is free."

These words, from Living, Loving, and Learning, by best-selling author Leo Buscaglia, provide an appropriate way to begin the stories of Sandra, Nancy, David, Sally, Tom, and Margie. They all share something in common. They are part of a larger group of more than 50 million Americans who consume more than 600 billion cigarettes each year (Surgeon General, The Health Consequences of Smoking: Nicotine Addiction, 1988).

There are probably many reasons people begin to smoke. However, for each smoker, these reasons are very personal. When asked why she started smoking, Sandra remembers distinctly. As a junior in high school, she felt compelled to join her cigarette smoking classmates. A personal crisis drove Nancy to cigarettes. David recalled that he felt very mature when, as a young man of 16, he started the cigarette habit he continued for 11 years. He doesn't remember exactly when he started, but he does remember he was following the lead of an older boy, his role model at the time. He certainly felt more comfortable around his "hero" when he imitated his cigarette habit, brand, and style of smoking. Sally remembers that she started smoking cigarettes regularly when she was a 16-year-old 11th grader. She started, along with a group of her friends, "to feel grown-up." Tom started his cigarette smoking habit of 36 years in high school. He felt very mature at the time, reason enough for one at the tender age of 17 to start. Almost 90% of all smokers started smoking in their teens

1

(Surgeon General, The Health Consequences of Smoking: Nicotine Addiction, 1988).

Margie doesn't remember the exact reasons she started smoking. She didn't have any difficulty, however, describing for a group of younger smokers what it means to have smoked for 39 years. While relating her smoking history to them, she asked, "Do you know how long 39 years is? It's now December of 1985 and I just had a birthday. The last time I had a birthday and was not a smoker was 1946." In what year did you celebrate your last birthday as a NONSMOKER?

Each of these individuals, plus Jack, Pep, Virginia, Tim, Joan, Karen, Ada, Alyce, and several hundred other people who have used the Cooper/ Clayton Method to stop smoking, had a background of heavy cigarette smoking for many years. At the time they started, we have no doubt that it seemed like a very "good" reason.

Although reasons for starting vary considerably, the reason most of them continued to smoke through the years is generally the same —they were hooked on nicotine. Smoking ceased to be a "casual" part of their lives. When they attempted to become nonsmokers, to withdraw from nicotine, their brain sent big bundles of hurt down on their body. This was done to punish them for even attempting a thing as ridiculous as denying the brain nicotine.

The people mentioned above, plus hundreds of others who have used the method described in this book, are now free of their previous dependence on nicotine. They are in control, not being controlled. Each has conquered his or her addiction of many years to nicotine.

TOM COOPER: A WINNER BUT NOT A QUITTER

Development of the Cooper/Clayton Method for Smoking Cessation begins with Tom and his struggles to become a nonsmoker. Tom is like many other smokers in this country. Perhaps you can identify with his story. We bet your story is not that much different.

Tom Cooper, like many heavy smokers, and like you, was successful in most of the things he attempted. If you asked people who know Tom to describe him, the following terms might be used — friendly, outgoing, organized, disciplined. He had a highly satisfactory family and professional life. In most of life's battles, Tom was a winner. Although every term listed above described Tom, there was one area where he wasn't a winner — smoking. Tom began smoking at age 17 and smoked regularly for 36 years. He first tried unsuccessfully to become a nonsmoker at age 22, failed again at age 27, then at age 32, ages 37, 42, 47, and 52. Based on his five year attempt/failure cycle, Tom was scheduled for another attempt to become a nonsmoker at age 57. Based on prior experience, he was also virtually "doomed to failure" again.

To someone who has never smoked, "doomed to failure" may sound harsh and be difficult to understand. Long-term smokers have no problem understanding. They are very much aware of the response of their brain when deprived of a drug it has come to expect on a regular basis. To them, the reason Tom failed in his attempts to become a nonsmoker is obvious. He was attempting to deny his brain, the control center of his entire being, a chemical agent it had enjoyed for 36 years. Each time he tried to deny his brain nicotine and failed, he was more hesitant about attempting AGAIN. He resolved to lay down his cigarettes many times, and tried. Good intentions, however, no matter how sincere, were never strong enough to overcome the pain he experienced. Therefore, he failed repeatedly.

On numerous occasions, Tom consciously refused to purchase cigarettes. He thought that if they weren't in the house, he couldn't smoke. Invariably he was wrong. Late at night, when he couldn't stand it anymore, he found himself searching ashtrays for a partially smoked cigarette butt. It didn't matter that it was dried out, brittle, and torn. A little clear plastic tape would make it smokable — at least smokable enough for a puff or two. He thus started again to feed his brain the nicotine it craved.

Some people become nonsmokers because of a dramatic event, possibly a heart attack, or because of the grim picture of life painted by their physician. However, nicotine exerts such a powerful hold on some people, even the fear of death is not enough to break that hold. Studies have shown that 30 to 60 percent of smokers return to cigarettes following a myocardial infarction (MI or "heart attack"). Tom Cooper was one of those. He experienced a heart attack at age 37. After spending 8 days in intensive care, one of the first things he sought out after being transferred to his hospital room was a cigarette. Needless to say, it didn't take long to return to his old pattern of smoking.

Tom knew that he was "hooked" on nicotine, that his was not just a psychological dependence. This is not to deny the importance of psychological factors in cigarette smoking. However, in Tom's case, and in the case of most heavy smokers, the psychological factors might be managed if there was not also the equally powerful physical dependence. Tom became aware of the power of the physical dependence factor the very first time he attempted to stop smoking at the tender age of 22. He still remembers the anguish from that and all other attempts to stop feeding nicotine to his brain. A few years later, Tom also became aware of another interesting phenomenon about nicotine. It occurred one summer while talking with a college student who was dating his sister. The young man and Tom would talk and smoke while waiting for Tom's sister to get ready for their date. Then, several days in a row, Tom noticed the young man didn't smoke. Upon being questioned by Tom he stated that, since his summer construction job began, he had lost his desire for cigarettes. He further explained he was working with an air operated jack hammer, breaking up the concrete floor of an old tobacco warehouse. The exhaust from the jack hammer stirred up tobacco dust which had collected on the concrete floors. He breathed fine particles of tobacco into his lungs all day long. Tom wondered if the young man lost his desire for cigarettes because the nicotine contained in the tobacco dust was satisfying his need for nicotine? It made sense to Tom that, regardless of the source of nicotine, if an individual were completely satiated with nicotine, the person would lose the desire to smoke. The brain must not be particular at all how it gets nicotine. It is only particular about getting its normal daily dose. Little did Tom realize how handy that information would prove to be some day.

Tom knew he introduced nicotine into his bloodstream by inhaling cigarette smoke into his lungs. He remembered that it takes only seven seconds for measurable levels of nicotine to travel from his lungs to his brain. In contrast, it would take over twice as long for a drug injected into a vein in his arm to reach his brain. Unfortunately, in order for Tom to get the nicotine he wanted from cigarettes, he had to burn the tobacco and inhale the smoke. He was thus pouring a large number of gasses into his lungs, one of which was carbon monoxide.

4

Tom also knew about carbon monoxide. He remembered that many commit suicide by connecting a hose to the tailpipe of their automobile and directing the exhaust fumes into a closed automobile. Carbon monoxide is an extremely dangerous gas. He also knew that when carbon monoxide is present, it reduces the ability of the blood to transport oxygen. Perhaps the best way to describe this is to think of a train station. Normally, oxygen is waiting in the lungs for the train (red blood cells) to come through. The smoker's lungs, however, contain both oxygen and carbon monoxide from the burning tobacco. The red blood cells will accept either the carbon monoxide or the oxygen as passengers. Unfortunately, the red blood cells are 200 times more likely to pick up the carbon monoxide than the oxygen. Once a red blood cell is linked with carbon monoxide, it gives it up very reluctantly. In the heavy smoker, as many as 10 to 15 percent of the red blood cells are tied up with carbon monoxide. This partially accounts for the shortness of breath experienced by heavy smokers.

TOM AND HIS PROMISE

For many years Tom had promised himself that, when he felt cigarette smoking was hurting him, he would become a nonsmoker. Intellectually he knew that the evidence overwhelmingly indicated smoking to be dangerous to health. However, he was able to rationalize that THEY — that nebulous group of "OTHERS" who smoked —were the ones toward whom the stop-smoking messages were directed. The messages weren't directed toward Tom. He didn't need to give up cigarettes because smoking was not hurting him, at least not yet. He was very successful in denying, at least to himself, that it was time for him to seriously address his 30-40 cigarettes-a-day problem. The reason he had started smoking, to feel so adult, had long ago disappeared.

A DAMASCUS ROAD EXPERIENCE IN
THE LOS ANGELES AIRPORT

One of the things that has changed most in human history is our ability to move quickly over great distances. During the first 1800 years AD, most people were born, grew up, married and had their own families, and died, within a relatively few miles of where they were born. The enlightening experiences of their lives had to take place "close to home." It is not surprising then to note that the pages of human history often focus on the explorers, those adventurers who traveled far from home and had miraculous experiences. Columbus, Pizzaro, Cortez, and others explored the New World. Marco Polo saw the riches of China and discovered societies, customs, and lands unknown to the Europeans. The apostle Paul traveled far and wide, and is credited with writing significant portions of the Christian New Testament. One of his enlightening experiences occurred on the road to Damascus. Although he was struck blind, he saw what he had never seen before, though it was there all the time.

An event, perhaps not as dramatic as the ones just described but seemingly as enlightening, occurred to Tom Cooper in the Los Angeles Airport. He had been in Anaheim to deliver a lecture at a meeting of the California Dental Association. While waiting for his flight home, Tom found himself seated across the aisle from a man about his age. Tom overheard the wife of the man arranging for her husband's in-flight oxygen supply. He was obviously incapable of breathing comfortably at high altitudes without assistance. While talking to the wife, Tom learned some frightening facts. One, the man had been a one and one-half to two packs a day smoker for 36 years, the same number of years that Tom had smoked about the same number of cigarettes. Two, the man suffered from COPD (Chronic Obstructive Pulmonary Disease). In this condition, chronic bronchitis is normally present. In addition, the air sacs in the lungs do not function properly. He could breath in, but had great difficulty exhaling. You see, emphysema is also a part of this crippling disease. If you have ever been around someone with this disease, frequently you discover yourself sympathetically attempting to breath for them. Tom asked the wife what life for her husband was like. The woman's answer made a deep impression on Tom. She said: "He's not living, he is only existing. Any quality of life he had is now gone."

A NEW RESOLVE AND A NEW ANSWER

Needless to say, Tom's flight home was not a relaxing experience. He couldn't get the man and his tortured breathing out of his mind. The woman's comments about the total lack of quality in the man's life bothered him greatly. The coincidence that Tom and the man were the same age, and had smoked the same number of cigarettes a day for 36 years, continued to creep back into his mind.

After arriving home, a second very unusual event occurred. At Tom's home, all of the new magazines seem to disappear before he gets a chance to glance at them. This is particularly true of *Reader's Digest*. In fact, Tom's turn to get *Reader's Digest* usually didn't occur until it had been in the house for two or three months. On this day however, he was the first person to get a chance to read the June 1984 copy of *Reader's Digest*. Glancing at the front cover, the title of an article by Walter Ross almost jumped off the page: "Nicotine Gum: The Drug That Helps Smokers Quit." The article explained that this product was a form of medication that contains nicotine. It could be used by smokers to assist them in giving up cigarettes. He thought to himself: "THIS IS THE ANSWER I HAVE BEEN LOOKING FOR."

In the first two months after the nicotine gum appeared on the market, there were 700,000 prescriptions written for it. A lot of people obviously felt a strong need to become nonsmokers. Tom Cooper was one of them.

Nicorette® (nicotine polacrilex) is marketed in the U.S. as a prescription medication.

Shortly thereafter, Tom picked up a prescription from his physician and had it filled at the pharmacy. He went home, opened the box, and read the instructions with great anticipation. Two of the instructions caused Tom to break out into a COLD SWEAT!

STARTING NOW YOU MUST GIVE UP SMOKING COMPLETELY. GRADUALLY CUTTING TOBACCO CONSUMPTION WILL NOT WORK.

WHENEVER YOU FEEL THAT YOU WANT TO SMOKE, PUT ONE PIECE OF GUM IN YOUR MOUTH.

Tom had tried to become a nonsmoker on many occasions and had failed. His previous attempts had taught him that cold turkey might make a delicious salad or sandwich, but it is a terribly painful way to discontinue a long-term pattern of heavy smoking. He wondered if this new way to give his brain nicotine would work.

From his pharmacology courses, Tom knew that any drug absorbed through the buccal mucosa or lining of the mouth would take over 10 minutes to arrive in measurable quantities in the brain. Compared to the seven seconds it takes for nicotine to reach the brain when cigarette smoke is inhaled, that is an eternity. Taking a piece of the nicotine gum when you feel that you want to smoke wouldn't work. He would be climbing the walls for a cigarette long before the nicotine could be absorbed through his cheek and reach the brain.

Digging back into his memory, Tom recalled a piece of information stored there one summer many years ago. He remembered his sister's friend who lost his desire for cigarettes. Tom recalled his thinking at the time. He had wondered if the young man was receiving all the nicotine his brain needed from the tobacco dust he inhaled while working in the old tobacco barn. He reasoned that, regardless of the source of the nicotine, keeping the nicotine blood level high will remove the desire for cigarettes. Finally, Tom knew that he was getting about 1 mg of nicotine per cigarette, and was smoking approximately one cigarette every 30 minutes. He was getting his nicotine on a very regular basis. He later found out that, typically, only about one mg of nicotine is extracted from a piece of 2 mg nicotine gum.

DEVELOPMENT OF THE
COOPER/CLAYTON METHOD

Tom was a heavy smoker. Tom reflected on how he started smoking some 36 years earlier. He recalled that he had added a few cigarettes at a time. He knew now from experience what he didn't know then. If he had tried smoking 30-40 cigarettes a day at the very beginning, he probably would have become ill from nicotine overdose. Even those first few cigarettes had made him nauseated. In essence, Tom had climbed a set of imaginary stair steps during the years he smoked. At each step he smoked more than previously. Each step was an increase in consumption. He had not jumped immediately from being a nonsmoker to his use of 30 to 40 cigarettes a day to feed his brain nicotine.

Tom concluded that the key to successfully giving up cigarettes was to CONTROL THE AMOUNT OF NICOTINE his brain received. The moral of the children's tale of the race between the tortoise and the hare seemed appropriate — slow and steady wins the race. After quick calculations, he realized that he had smoked a total of 1,872 weeks (36 years x 52 weeks). On all prior attempts to become a nonsmoker, Tom had been anxious for instant signs of success. This time would be different. It was clear to Tom that the key was in SLOWLY reducing the body's dependence on nicotine. The instructions in the nicotine gum package indicated that the use of the nicotine gum for longer than six months had not been adequately studied, so he thought a person should not use the medication continuously for longer than six months. Tom decided to use six months as the period during which he would take control of his dependence on nicotine. Your doctor will decide what dosage regimen is right for you. In one way, six months seemed like a long time. However, compared to the 432 months he had spent developing his smoking pattern, six months was a very short period. While there was an urgency this time to overcome his nicotine dependence, there was an even greater need to be successful — to be a "winner" this time — to become a permanent nonsmoker.

TOM THE TEACHER

Tom knew that before he started smoking, his brain had not craved nicotine. He had taught his brain to want it. He reasoned that what he had taught his brain, he could also unteach it. He had chosen to become a smoker, he could also choose to become a nonsmoker. His brain, during all the years before he started smoking cigarettes, thought zero nicotine each day was normal. Tom reasoned that, to remain a nonsmoker permanently, he must teach his brain to accept smaller and smaller amounts of nicotine as normal. The final step would teach his brain, once again, that zero nicotine is normal. Only then would he win his battle with cigarettes.

The drug contained in the nicotine gum is the same drug Tom was getting from cigarettes. The key difference is the way nicotine (1) enters the body and, (2) how long it takes for it to reach the brain. The brain of a heavy smoker has been trained to expect a steady dosing schedule of nicotine. Whenever the blood level of nicotine is reduced to a certain point, the brain starts screaming for more. This has been referred to as the body's "nicostat" that operates much like a thermostat operates in your home to regulate temperature. It tells the smoker when additional nicotine is needed to maintain adequate blood levels. Research on nicotine indicates that persons who are allowed to receive nicotine through an IV drip lose most of their craving for cigarettes. Other research subjects, when allowed to press either a key which released nicotine, or one which released sterile water into their veins, learned rapidly which key gave them the nicotine. They were then able to release nicotine into the blood stream on a regular basis.

Tom reasoned that the level of nicotine in his blood had to be kept high enough so that his body's "nicostat" would never start screaming for nicotine. The package insert for the 2 mg nicotine gum indicated that the maximum daily allowance was 30 pieces. This seemed totally adequate from Tom's perspective. After all, he was getting about 30 mg of nicotine a day from his cigarettes. He had to give his brain enough nicotine initially to satisfy its needs, but would limit the source of nicotine to the nicotine gum.

Tom also knew that using the nicotine gum like chewing gum would result in the nicotine being released too rapidly. As a dentist, he knew that chewing increases the amount of saliva in the mouth. Finally, he knew that the excess saliva which contained the nicotine released from the nicotine gum, would cause him to swallow. The nicotine that would be swallowed was lost for practical purposes. It was essential that he keep the released nicotine in the mouth long enough to allow absorption into his blood. As a dentist, Tom knew that chewing the nicotine gum would not only cause an increase in the flow of saliva, with increased saliva would come more frequent swallowing. This would result in most of the nicotine being swallowed, rather than remaining in the mouth where it could be absorbed through the cheek. Thus, he decided to hold the nicotine gum in his mouth between the cheek and gum.

The questions that remained to be answered were: how often should he take the nicotine gum and, how much of it should be taken? Being a very organized and disciplined individual, Tom decided first to chart his smoking patterns. The best way to know how much of the nicotine gum to use was to determine how often and when he smoked. Therefore, for two weeks, Tom recorded every cigarette he smoked, and when he smoked it. Why two weeks? Tom felt that 2 weeks were required for him to become acutely aware of his smoking patterns and to build up his commitment to become a nonsmoker. He felt he also needed to know what times of the day his smoking was the heaviest. What he learned was very interesting. He smoked a very consistent number of cigarettes, in a consistent pattern, at consistent times.

Tom's use of the nicotine gum as a replacement source of nicotine, he reasoned, would involve use of nicotine gum in the same pattern he followed when getting his nicotine from cigarettes. In an "ad lib" or "as needed" dosage pattern, the patient sets the dosage rate and amount. He would only change the way he supplied his brain with nicotine.

One of the ways that the Cooper/Clayton Method has changed since its development in 1984 is to include the latest nicotine replacement technology. In November of 1991, the Food and Drug Administration allowed a new skin patch containing nicotine to be marketed. Nicoderm® (nicotine transdermal system) is the trade name for this patch which is marketed by Marion Merrell Dow Inc. of Kansas City, Missouri. This is the same company responsible for marketing the nicotine gum, Nicorette® (nicotine polacrilex). Nicoderm is a nicotine patch which is worn on the surface of the skin. This patch releases nicotine through the skin (transdermal). This nicotine goes into the blood and reaches the brain to help relieve withdrawal symptoms when cigarettes are no longer used as the individual's source of nicotine.

As an aid to your comprehensive behavioral smoking-cessation program, Nicoderm, will become your new and ONLY source of nicotine. Your physician or dentist will assist you to choose the appropriate starting dosage of nicotine from Nicoderm, which will be your new and only source of nicotine for the next few weeks. You will also be taught how to gently reduce your nicotine intake until your brain accepts zero nicotine as normal. We encourage you to seek out a group smoking-cessation program near you to enjoy the additional benefits of group interaction.

THE PROGRAM

The Cooper/Clayton Method for Smoking Cessation evolved and emerged out of Tom Cooper's determination to be victorious over cigarettes, smoking, and nicotine. It has been refined since then by the experiences of hundreds of heavy smokers. These former smokers eliminated nicotine from their lives by following the steps described briefly below, and in detail in the following chapters of this book. Figure 2.1 is a chart outlining the total program. By referring to this chart, you will be able to locate where you are, review where you have been, and know where you are going during each of the 24 weeks of the Cooper/Clayton Method.

The addition of the transdermal patch, Nicoderm® (nicotine transdermal system), adds significantly to our arsenal of weapons in helping you become a nonsmoker. The steps of the Cooper/Clayton Method remain the same; the addition of Nicoderm provides an opportunity to "tailor" the Method to your need for nicotine while you also address the important social and psychological factors involved in your smoking.

STEPS IN THE COOPER/CLAYTON METHOD

STEP 1. QUALIFICATION (2 WEEKS)

During this step, each cigarette you smoke will be recorded. This will show you the total number of cigarettes you smoke each day and your pattern of smoking in connection with other activities. You will determine the amount of nicotine your brain expects as "normal."

STEP 2. SUBSTITUTION AND MAINTENANCE I (6-8 WEEKS)

During this step, you will change the way your body receives its daily supply of nicotine. Day 1 of this period, and thereafter, you will use Nicoderm instead of the cigarettes you formerly smoked. Your physician or dentist will determine the nicotine content of the transdermal patch you will use during this 6-8 week period. Nicoderm should provide enough nicotine to keep your body's blood nicotine high enough to prevent your craving cigarettes. You, as a former smoker, will train your brain to accept less nicotine than previously received from cigarettes. During this period you should be involved in a comprehensive behavioral smoking-cessation program. This will significantly improve your chances to become a nonsmoker.

STEP 3. ELIMINATION I AND MAINTENANCE II (2-4 WEEKS)

During this step, the amount of nicotine you receive from Nicoderm will be reduced, by switching to a patch that is smaller in size and contains less nicotine. You will continue using this patch daily for 2-4 weeks, to allow more time for you to distance yourself from smoking and cigarettes, and to provide more time for you to adjust the other aspects of your life associated with smoking. During the two to four weeks in this step, the daily intake of nicotine from Nicoderm is maintained at the new reduced level. The brain soon accepts this reduced level of nicotine as "normal." Your continued involvement in a comprehensive behavioral smoking-cessation program will help you make other adjustments as you learn to live as a nonsmoker.

STEP 4. ELIMINATION II (2-4 WEEKS)

During this step, you will again reduce the amount of nicotine you receive daily. You will wear a still smaller patch for 2-4 weeks which delivers about one-third the nicotine you received from the first patch.   Our goal is to help you become a nonsmoker permanently by breaking your dependence on nicotine, regardless of the source. Your brain will eventually accept zero nicotine as normal. Your brain will have been trained to function without any nicotine. The support you receive from your comprehensive behavioral smoking-cessation program will continue to provide the help you need to complete this phase of your transition from smoker to nonsmoker.

Please Note:

Your physician or dentist may determine you should start your medication with the 14 mg Nicoderm patch. In that case, your dosage and time schedule can be altered by your prescribing doctor.

STEP 5. RELAPSE PREVENTION (6-12 WEEKS)

During this period you will receive positive reinforcement about your decision to become a nonsmoker. You will realize your needs are met more completely by remaining a nonsmoker. You will learn strategies to cope with stress, anger, and depression without nicotine. Your chances for long-term success will be increased if you continue as a member of a support group composed of individuals who share your commitment to remain a nonsmoker.

VICTORY OVER A MAJOR FOE

Tom followed a similar method using the nicotine gum. It wasn't a "piece of cake," but THIS time Tom Cooper was successful in becoming a nonsmoker. He taught his brain to survive without nicotine, just as he had taught it 36 years earlier how to live with and "expect" nicotine. Tom had won a major battle in his life. He had taken control over what had previously controlled him.

Tom's last cigarette was on May 29, 1984. He was completely off the nicotine gum by November 19, 1984. Tom enjoyed being a nonsmoker, privately satisfied with total victory at last. He learned that life has a way of calming down after major battles are over.

The method he followed was set aside, much as one would do with a plaque or certificate or trophy received for a "job well done." It was there, not forgotten, but it didn't get much attention.

YOU DID IT. CAN YOU HELP ME?

Tom's actions had not gone unobserved. Sandra, who attended the same church as Tom, was watching. She was a successful nurse, wife, mother, and had been a smoker for 31 years. She had tried to become a nonsmoker 18 years earlier. She participated in a smoking-cessation program operated as part of the hospital's health promotion emphasis. It was a terrible experience. Sandra said that she made herself one promise after that experience: "I'll never try to give up cigarettes again."

14

She enjoyed smoking, but felt she needed to become a nonsmoker. At the same time, based on her previous experience, she was terrified at the thought of even trying. Sandra knew Tom only casually. She didn't feel comfortable just walking up and asking him to help her. Therefore, she wrote Tom a letter asking him to help her become a nonsmoker. Having mailed the letter, she knew she was committed.

Tom pulled his records from the shelf, dusted them off, and began to systematically review what he had gone through almost a year earlier. Sandra vowed to use the method exactly as Tom described it. She didn't want the method to be her excuse if she failed. When Sandra had completed the Qualification and Substitution/Maintenance Steps, she encouraged Tom to help others who might be interested in becoming nonsmokers. At that time Tom asked Dick Clayton to help him. Dick, an expert in the area of drug abuse, had provided weekly advice and help to Tom as he became a nonsmoker and had been doing the same with Sandra. An announcement was made from the pulpit of Centenary United Methodist Church in Lexington, Ky. The first group would meet on the following Wednesday night. All smokers who wanted or needed to become nonsmokers were invited. Those who had tried to give up cigarettes on a number of prior occasions were especially encouraged to attend. Tom, Sandra, and Dick were joined by a number of people. Since then, hundreds of persons have benefited from the Cooper/Clayton Method. It worked for them. It can work for you.

WHY DOES THE COOPER/CLAYTON METHOD WORK?

It works because it makes sense. Over the years you increased the amount of nicotine you provided your brain each hour of the day. Step by step, you taught your brain to expect larger amounts of nicotine each day as "normal." To successfully withdraw nicotine from the brain, to reduce nicotine slowly as you go back down the stairs, also makes sense. You can teach your brain to accept smaller and smaller amounts as "normal" until its final expectation is that zero nicotine is normal.

Also, the environment in which you taught yourself to smoke probably encouraged smoking. Advertising was very effective in convincing you that the "in" thing was to smoke cigarettes. Smoking was presented as a glamorous, success-oriented, pleasure-associated addition to your life.

To look at the environment in which you smoke today is to observe predominantly negative reactions to smoking cigarettes. These negative forces include the Surgeon General's Reports, a flood of negative articles in newspapers and popular magazines, and an increasing number of public places in which cigarette smoking is banned.

Why does the Cooper/Clayton Method to Become a Nonsmoker work? It works because the Method is right and the Time is right.

REVIEW OF THE DEVELOPMENT OF THE COOPER/CLAYTON METHOD

This program was developed to enable a heavy smoker to rid himself of an undesirable cigarette problem. It involves a comprehensive behavioral smoking-cessation program and adjunct pharmacologic replacement therapy of an alternate nicotine source for your cigarettes. It then slowly and gently reduces the alternate source of nicotine to zero as you continue to learn during your participation in the behavioral program to face your world without nicotine.

It is not fancy.

It involves no magic.

It requires only ONE commitment on your part: to tackle YOUR smoking problem one HOUR at a time, one DAY at a time.

If you initially chose to smoke, you now have the opportunity to choose NOT to smoke.

The Cooper/Clayton Method will provide you with the means to take control of the cigarettes that previously controlled you. Hundreds have used this Method to regain that control. We now want to share it with you.

16

CHAPTER 2

ADMISSION

Many words in the English language have a common spelling but more than one meaning. In order to understand the meaning, you have to understand how the word is used. One such word is admission. Webster's New Collegiate Dictionary lists several definitions of ADMISSION. The two that apply here are:

1. the act or process of admitting.

2. acknowledgment that a fact or statement is true.

THE ACT OR PROCESS OF ADMITTING.

It is sometimes difficult for an adult to admit any weakness. In our society, as in most, to admit a weakness is to leave oneself open to criticism.

ACKNOWLEDGMENT THAT A FACT OR STATEMENT IS TRUE.

During the first step in the Cooper/Clayton Method to Become a Nonsmoker, you will be asked to record each cigarette you smoke over a two-week period. This is not a childish exercise. Our research has shown that people who are unwilling to make this commitment are still denying the seriousness of their smoking patterns. Frequently, they are kidding themselves about their desire to become a nonsmoker.

PLEASE NOTE:

In our clinical practice and in this book, our focus is on BECOMING A NONSMOKER. We always ask smokers: would you like to become a

NONSMOKER? We seldom meet a smoker whose answer to this question is No. Throughout this book we will refer to becoming a nonsmoker.

Therefore, you hold the key. While we will guide and assist you, we want to make it absolutely clear that at no time in this program will we focus on your weaknesses. We all have them. Neither will we criticize you for your dependence on cigarettes and nicotine. The Cooper/Clayton Method is not built on negative or critical principles. Instead, it is built on the principle that problems can be solved by first recognizing that they are real, not imaginary, and second by recognizing that the only person who can solve or tackle a problem is the person who owns it.

If you are a cigarette smoker and have had difficulty becoming a nonsmoker, you have a problem. The first step in dealing with any problem is to admit that it is a problem.

ARE YOU READY FOR ADMISSION?

We ask you to acknowledge and recognize, that is, admit, five factors or five facts as you begin the process of becoming a nonsmoker.

1. ADMIT YOU ENJOY SMOKING

Don't lie to yourself by saying something like: "I really don't like smoking." Of course you do. The next time you light up your first cigarette of the morning, watch yourself in the mirror. Be aware of how deeply you inhale the smoke. Be aware of the sense of comfort that first cigarette of the day provides. You enjoy smoking and it's okay to admit it. We have never met a smoker who didn't enjoy smoking and who really, seriously, would not prefer to continue smoking. For some reason they feel they "have to" or "ought to" or "need to" become a nonsmoker. Down deep, where they really live and can be honest with themselves, they don't want to change. That is nothing to be ashamed of. Smoking is probably more a part of your life than you are aware.

However, there are some aspects of smoking that all smokers, if they are truly honest with themselves, must admit are not much fun. We have listed a few of these below. We aren't asking you to keep score, but do be honest with yourself in answering these questions.

• Do you really enjoy holding a burning object between your fingers? If your answer is Yes, what is there about this act that provides satisfaction?

• Do you really enjoy smoke causing your eyes to water? If the cigarette were cabbage leaves, and contained no nicotine, would you still irritate your eyes with a burning "cabbage stick?"

• Have you ever dropped a lighted cigarette into your lap while sitting in a nice chair or while driving? Do you really enjoy such an experience?

• Have you noticed burn holes in your clothes caused by hot cigarette ash? Have you ever ruined a favorite suit or dress because of these little side effects of smoking?

• Do you find ashtrays attractive when they are piled high? How do you like the sight of an overflowing ashtray in the morning before you've had your shower and morning juice? Do you really enjoy looking at the dead butts and piles of ashes you produce? Be honest.

• What about the smell of stale tobacco smoke in your hair, on your clothes, on your breath? Do you enjoy that smell? Do you think other people enjoy it?

You probably started smoking for "social" reasons. Perhaps it was the influence of your friends who were smoking. Maybe the idea that smoking would make you appear older and more mature appealed to you. The first cigarettes you smoked probably made you nauseated. Nevertheless, you continued to smoke. As the number of cigarettes you smoked increased, the kind of enjoyment provided by smoking changed. Instead of smoking for social reasons, you began to smoke because it made you feel different. You enjoyed smoking because it made you feel energetic when you were down, and relaxed when you were anxious or under pressure. To the social reasons, you could now add the psychological dependence that developed over a period of time. Following this, a physical dependence also became evident, as your brain receptor sites were trained to expect larger and larger amounts of nicotine. Smokers eventually come to realize that a major reason they continue to smoke is because THEY HAVE TO. If they try to deny their brain nicotine, they feel miserable. The only thing that relieves the misery is smoking. Has this been your experience? You aren't alone.

2. ADMIT YOU CAN'T GIVE UP SMOKING EASILY

Don't claim that: "I can give up smoking anytime I want to." Virtually every long-term smoker has tried to stop on a number of occasions, and has been successful, but for relatively short periods. Some stop smoking for a whole day each year in celebration of the "Great American Smoke Out." A few stop smoking in conjunction with surgery or a hospital stay. Others stop smoking while they are pregnant. The fact is, many smokers try to become a nonsmoker permanently and are unable to. The reason they can't give up cigarettes is that they are addicted to nicotine. Now this may seem like a rather harsh statement to you, but stay with us. Admitting that you are addicted to nicotine may be extremely important in your battle to become a nonsmoker.

English researchers, M.A.H. Russell and M.J. Jarvis have the following to say about nicotine and its role in the continuation of smoking.

People smoke cigarettes for many reasons — social, psychological, sensory, behavioral, and pharmacological. But of all of these the pharmacological reasons are the most powerful and the most fundamental. If tobacco contained no nicotine, there would be no problem. People wouldn't smoke it, nor would they snuff it or chew it.

Simply put, most people smoke because they are addicted to nicotine. The "social" and "psychological" factors are also present. They help in solidifying the role that smoking plays in a person's life. However, the most important factor in smoking is physiological. You continue to smoke because your brain has developed a dependence on nicotine. An admission of this fact is central to successfully winning the battle over smoking cigarettes.

ARE SMOKERS ADDICTED?

Dr. Jerome Jaffe is a psychiatrist and one of the world's leading experts on drug addiction. Much of his earlier research dealt with the opiates, such as heroin. In recent years, he has devoted a great deal of time to the problem of dependence on nicotine. Dr. Jaffe is the former Director of the Addiction Research Center of the National Institute on Drug Abuse, located in Baltimore. He says that "addiction" has three important elements: (1) an overwhelming involvement with the drug; (2) time spent in securing the drug; and (3) a high potential for returning to the drug after the individual has been successful in giving it up.

Overwhelming Involvement With Use of a Drug

Any smoker will testify to this aspect of smoking. Cigarettes are often handled with greater care than one would handle valuable crystal or china. The smoker's day revolves around smoking. Meetings involving smokers usually include smoking breaks. When asked a question, smokers often "buy time" to think with a set pattern of action. First they pull a package of cigarettes out of their pocket or purse. Then, taking a cigarette out of the pack, they tap it on the table. They continue the almost sacred ritual by lighting it and taking a deep puff. Finally, after all of that, they are ready to answer the question. Are you addicted? You are the expert on your smoking. You know from experience about the degree to which your life revolves around smoking.

Securing a Supply of a Drug

Smokers cannot afford to be smug when they hear about heroin addicts and the lengths they go to get a supply of the drug. Have you ever gone out in a driving rainstorm or blizzard because you were out of cigarettes? Have you ever gotten up in the middle of the night, realized you needed a cigarette, and panicked because you couldn't find any in the house? Have you ever gone to a closet and fished in the pockets of coats or jackets to find an old package with one remaining cigarette? Upon inhaling the smoke from that brittle, dry, old cigarette, you found it was so strong it made your hair stand on end? We bet you smoked it anyway. Have there been times when you would have done almost anything for a cigarette? If you can answer Yes to some or all of these questions, you are probably addicted to nicotine. Don't be ashamed. There are 50 million plus smokers in the United States alone. Like you, most of them have had these types of experiences. They too may be addicted to nicotine.

High Relapse After Withdrawal

One of the things that cuts across all forms of drug dependence/addiction is the terrible hold drugs have over their victims. Among heroin addicts there is a belief: "Once addicted, always addicted." The same belief is held by many smokers. A large number of smokers stop smoking each year, then return to smoking after a period of abstinence. Virtually all smokers have tried to eliminate cigarettes at least once. Most have tried on more than one occasion. Many found they could be successful, but only temporarily. Have you previously tried to stop smoking and failed? More than one attempt and more than one failure? Are you somewhat embarrassed to attempt again, and risk failure again?

The smoking-cessation method described in this book is designed for those who have tried to become nonsmokers, and have failed. It is for those who feel a need to become a nonsmoker, for whatever reasons, and are willing to make a commitment. This Method is for smokers who are sick and tired of being controlled by cigarettes, smokers who are tired of the embarrassment that comes from going through ashtrays looking for old butts to smoke. This Method is for smokers who want to become nonsmokers, smokers who want to win their battle with nicotine and cigarettes.

3. ADMIT NOT BECOMING A NONSMOKER IS NOT ENTIRELY YOUR FAULT

Don't be too hard on yourself because you haven't been able to become a nonsmoker. What you probably don't know is that nicotine is very addicting. The Surgeon General's Report (1988:iii) stated that: "Careful examination of the data makes it clear that cigarettes and other forms of tobacco are addicting. An extensive body of research has shown that nicotine is the drug in tobacco that causes addiction. Moreover, the processes that determine tobacco addiction are similar to those that determine addiction to drugs such as heroin and cocaine." It is no wonder you haven't been successful in the past in your attempts to become a nonsmoker. Breaking an addiction to nicotine is extremely difficult. You might ask: "Why is this so?" The answer lies in how nicotine is provided to the brain.

When you smoke a cigarette, you inhale the smoke and nicotine into your lungs. The efficiency of introducing a drug through the lungs is one reason cigarette smoking is so difficult a dependence to treat. Any substance absorbed into the blood through the lungs: (a) bypasses one-half of the circulatory system; and (b) takes just seven seconds to reach the brain. This is a shorter period of time than it takes any other drug, including heroin injected directly into a vein in the arm or leg, to reach the brain.

The brain is an incredibly complex organ. It is able to sort substances put into the body into categories, and then dispatch those substances to the specific areas of the brain that are naturally responsive to them. These areas are called receptor sites. Once activated, they are very sensitive to blood nicotine levels, and get trained quickly to want more and more nicotine. The brain of a heavy smoker has more receptor sites than that of a light smoker (Surgeon General, The Health Consequences of Smoking: Nicotine Addiction, 1988, page 92). When a person smokes, the nicotine from the cigarette can be thought of as a gift one is presenting to the brain. The brain is quickly spoiled, and begins to demand the gift of nicotine on a very regular schedule. If you think that is not so, try giving up smoking and nicotine abruptly — cold turkey.

Without nicotine, the brain says to the rest of the body — "I'm being deprived of something I want. I am going to make other parts of your body miserable until I receive what I want. Give me some nicotine." You crave tobacco, begin to get irritable, you begin to gain weight, you think of nothing but smoking. Then, you surrender. You give the spoiled brat what it craves. Once the brain, mother nature's thermostat, gets what it wants, you are allowed some peace. Notice how quickly you return to your previous pattern of smoking.

This pattern of rewarding the brain with the nicotine it wants, when it wants it, is known by scientists as "reinforcement." Let's briefly compare the "reinforcement" or "rewarding" process that occurs for persons addicted to heroin and those addicted to nicotine. Most heroin addicts spend time each year in jails, hospitals, and/or treatment centers. The typical heroin addict thus ends up using heroin on a daily basis about 250 days out of the year (see Nurco, Ball, Shaffer, and Hanlon, "The criminality of narcotic addicts," Journal of Nervous and Mental Disease, Vol. 173 (1985), 94-102). On those days when the addict is using heroin, the chances are good that the drug will be used no more than five times a day. In comparison, think about how often you use nicotine. If you are a pack and a half smoker, your brain receives a reward of nicotine at least 30 times a day.

But, wait a minute. You don't just take one puff on each cigarette. You take a number of puffs. At the rate of 10 puffs per cigarette, the smoker averaging 30 cigarettes per day takes about 109,500 puffs a year. Most smokers with whom we work use cigarettes 365 days a year, day in and day out. They smoke when they have a bad cold, when they have the flu, when they are sick. In fact, there is no other mood-altering drug that smokers more regularly and consistently take into the body than nicotine.

4. ADMIT YOU NEED HELP

It is important to recognize that you may need help in becoming a nonsmoker. You probably know some people who have had a relatively easy time giving up cigarettes. Perhaps they are your family or close friends. Perhaps they used the cold turkey approach and were successful. When you tried the same technique, you failed. If someone else can do it "on their own" and you can't, DON'T WORRY ABOUT IT. There are millions of people just like you who want to become nonsmokers, but just haven't been able to do it. We are delighted for those who have been successful without any assistance. They don't need our help. The Method described in this book is designed for those who have not been so fortunate. It has proved successful for people who have tried other techniques and strategies, and have failed. You need to ADMIT that you need help. This book, as a part of a comprehensive behavioral smoking-cessation program can provide that help.

5. ADMIT YOU NEED A PLAN

We want you to follow through on your admission that you need help. The Method that is described in Chapters 3, 4, 5, and 6 of this book can provide that help. The Cooper/Clayton Method is simple to follow. It makes sense. It doesn't require superhuman effort. It is something you can do for yourself. If you plan your work and work your plan, you will be successful in practically any area of life. This is particularly true with regard to becoming a nonsmoker.

REVIEW OF ADMISSION TO
THE COOPER/CLAYTON METHOD

The Cooper/Clayton Method can help you to become a nonsmoker. It is based on the fact that nicotine is an addicting drug. Now that you know this, you shouldn't be surprised that you, along with millions of other smokers, have had such a difficult time becoming a nonsmoker. Nicotine is hard to give up because it is a reward your brain has come to expect, day-in and day-out.

As you begin the process of becoming a nonsmoker, review these five criteria for ADMISSION. YOU decide if you want to continue to the next step in the Cooper/Clayton Method. Briefly, the criteria are:

1. **ADMIT YOU ENJOY SMOKING.**

2. **ADMIT YOU CAN'T GIVE UP SMOKING EASILY.**

3. **ADMIT NOT BECOMING A NONSMOKER IS NOT ENTIRELY YOUR FAULT.**

4. **ADMIT YOU NEED HELP.**

5. **ADMIT YOU NEED A PLAN.**

The remainder of this book contains a sensible and workable plan for you. Just as hundreds have done, let our plan become your plan. Your plan will work, however, only if you follow it!

Are you ready? Fine, let's begin.

The Cooper / Clayton Method

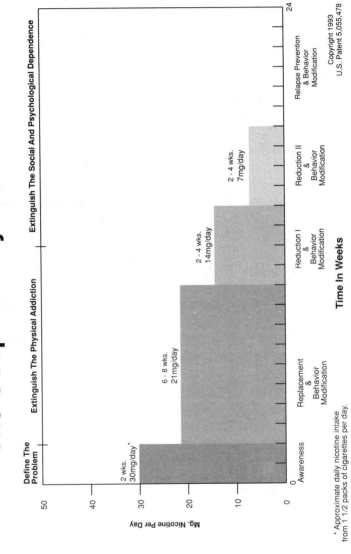

Figure 2-1

26

CHAPTER 3

STEP 1. QUALIFICATION

A Chinese philosopher, Lao Tse, is credited with the famous saying: "Every journey of a thousand miles begins with the first step." The simple message in this ancient saying remains just as true today. Before you can walk, you must crawl. Before you speak in sentences, you use single words. Every book starts with the first word. A journey is not really a journey; it is a series of short trips.

We are going to assist you in taking a journey. Before any journey can begin, however, some basic planning must occur. You must determine:

1. The Origin of Your Journey

2. The Destination You Have Chosen

3. The Travel Plan You Will Follow

4. The Reward Plan You Have Developed

The ORIGIN of each smoker's journey to becoming a nonsmoker is unique. One person may smoke 30 cigarettes which are rated very high in nicotine. A second may smoke 30 cigarettes rated relatively low in nicotine. You could reasonably expect their respective journeys to differ dramatically. The difference, you hypothesize, will result from the varying amounts of nicotine which their brains have come to expect. Do not be surprised, however, if this expectation does not materialize. In all probability, you and your smoking friends who smoke comparable numbers of cigarettes have nicotine needs which are very similar. This can occur because some people are "more efficient" smokers. They get significant amounts of nicotine from "low nicotine" cigarettes by inhaling more deeply and for longer periods of time. The individual who smokes the "high nicotine" content cigarette does not have to work so hard to get the same amount of nicotine.

Research has shown that a smoker changes both the number of cigarettes smoked and inhalation patterns as different cigarettes are provided. In one study, conducted by Dr. Neal Benowitz, smokers did not know what "strength" cigarettes they were provided. They increased the number of cigarettes smoked when given "mild" cigarettes and decreased the number smoked when "stronger" cigarettes were provided. They did this in order to maintain comfortable blood nicotine levels, regardless of the "strength" of cigarettes they smoked.

In spite of the number of cigarettes smoked or the nicotine content, the DESTINATION of all cigarette smokers who have made a commitment to stop smoking cigarettes is the same. They have chosen to become NONSMOKERS! That is the end point of this journey.

The TRAVEL PLAN is the course of action necessary to take you from where you are now (a smoker) to where you choose to be (a nonsmoker).

The REWARD PLAN will involve anticipation of the many benefits you will receive at journey's end. You logically expect some fun and pleasure upon completion of any journey. Why should this trip be different? We will concentrate in this book on the REWARDS you receive when you BECOME A NONSMOKER, rather than ALL THE BAD THINGS that happen to people who CONTINUE SMOKING.

This step in the travel plan for the Cooper/Clayton Method is called QUALIFICATION. It takes only 2 weeks to complete, but requires a commitment from you. When you make the commitment during these two weeks to follow the Method, you will qualify yourself to begin the Method.

There obviously are other plans to help you become a nonsmoker. Many of those other plans work. For those who have used those plans and succeeded, congratulations. To those who are more heavily dependent on nicotine and did not succeed with other plans, there is hope. You are not a failure. You are not weak. You are addicted to a powerful drug. You may need the plan described in this book to rid yourself of your addiction. There may be ways to modify this Method. We don't know how a modification will work. We DO KNOW this Method works as it is described in this book. When you use this plan, we urge you to follow it and not attempt to rewrite it.

Hundreds who have allowed us to share this Method with them have succeeded. They have become nonsmokers. We didn't become nonsmokers for them — they did so for themselves. We can't become a nonsmoker for you, but you will be able to become a nonsmoker for yourself. We want to help you to be successful. Therefore, let us begin with the FIRST STEP in what may be the most important journey you've ever taken.

THE ORIGIN OF THE JOURNEY: WHERE ARE YOU NOW?

The purpose of the first step is to find out where you are as a smoker. This involves answering some questions.

QUESTION 1. HOW IMPORTANT IS SMOKING IN YOUR LIFE?

The way this question is asked is very similar to a technique used widely by sociologists and psychologists for measuring a person's self-esteem or self-concept. A person is asked to write down the first 10 things that come to mind in response to the question: "Who Am I?" The person will usually list several very general characteristics such as:

> male/female
> age
> marital status
> parental status
> job/profession
> education achieved

Then, the writer will begin to get more personal, listing specific traits such as:

> ambitious
> athletic
> handsome/beautiful
> charming

If we asked you to list 10 words to describe yourself, you might list any or all of the above. When you continued to select words to describe yourself, would CIGARETTE SMOKER appear on your list? How important is smoking to you? It may be one of the most costly and time-consuming activities in which you are involved.

Dr. Karl-Olov Fagerstrom, a leading expert on nicotine dependence from Sweden, has devised a test to determine how important cigarette smoking is to an individual. Let's see how you do on the test.

****

DR. FAGERSTROM'S QUESTIONS

****

1. How soon after you wake in the morning   YOUR SCORE
    do you smoke your first cigarette?
    a. within 30 minutes ....= 1
    b. more than 30 minutes ....= 0   _____

2. Do you find it difficult not to smoke where smoking is forbidden?
    a. Yes .... = 1
    b. No..= 0   _____

3. Which of all of the cigarettes you smoke during the day is the most
    satisfying?
    a. First one in the morning ....= 1
    b. Any other ....= 0   _____

4. How many cigarettes do you smoke a day?
    a. 1-15, light smoker ....= 0
    b. 16-25, moderate smoker ....= 1
    c. 25 or more, heavy smoker ....= 2   _____

5. Do you smoke more in the morning than the rest of the day?
   a. Yes .... = 1
   b. No.. = 0   _____

6. Do you smoke when you are sick enough to have to stay in bed?
   a. Yes ....= 1
   b. No..= 0   _____

7. What is the tar/nicotine rating of the brand you smoke?
   a. low tar, 1-8 mgs ....= 0
   b. medium tar, 9-15 mgs ....= 1
   c. high tar, 15 or more mgs ....= 2   _____

8. How often do you inhale?
   a. Occasionally ....= 0
   b. Often ....= 1
   c. Always ....= 2   _____

Highest Possible Score = 11 .... Your Score _____

****

Well, how did you do? If your score is zero, your level of dependence on cigarettes is not very strong. The higher your score is, 1 to 11, the more strongly addicted you are to nicotine. The more addicted you are to nicotine, the more difficulty you would probably experience in going cold turkey. Remember, the Cooper/Clayton Method does not involve going cold turkey. It only changes your SOURCE of nicotine, then gently reduces the new source to zero at a comfortable, manageable rate.

Dr. Fagerstrom's questions are interesting in that they ask you where you are NOW. The following section will help you understand how important smoking has been to you in the past.

COMPARE YOURSELF TO ANOTHER SMOKER

To illustrate how the following questions work, we're reporting answers that were given to us by Tom. We want you to fill in the blanks on the right side of the page to show your smoking patterns.

31

1. How old were you when you first started smoking cigarettes regularly?

TOM'S ANSWER: <u>17</u>   YOUR ANSWER: _____

2. How old are you now?

TOM'S ANSWER: <u>53</u>   YOUR ANSWER: _____

3. Calculate the total years you smoked.

TOM'S ANSWER: <u>53-17 = 36</u>   YOUR ANSWER: _____

4. How many cigarettes a day did you usually smoke during those years?

TOM'S ANSWER: <u>30 a day.</u>   YOUR ANSWER: _____

5. Calculate the total number of cigarettes you have smoked.

TOM'S ANSWER: YOUR ANSWER:
30 per day x 365 days =   _____ per day x 365 days =
10,950 per year   _____ per year

10,950 x 36 years =   _____ x _____ years =
394,200 cigarettes   _____ cigarettes
during lifetime   during lifetime.

6. Calculate the total number of times you inhaled a cigarette (Remember: Each time you inhaled a cigarette, you sent a measurable "hit" of nicotine to your brain. A typical smoker inhales each cigarette 10 times).

TOM'S ANSWER: YOUR ANSWER:
394,200 cigarettes x   _____ cigarettes x
10 inhalations =   10 inhalations =
3,942,000 "hits" of nicotine   _____ "hits" of nicotine
to smoker's brain   to your brain.

7. A typical "burn time" for a cigarette is about 5 minutes. Calculate how much time you have spent with a cigarette lit.

TOM'S ANSWER: YOUR ANSWER:
394,200 x 5 minutes =   _____ x 5 minutes =
1,971,000 minutes burn time   _____ minutes burn time

1,971,000 divided by 60 =	_____ divided by 60 =
32,850 hours burn time	_____ hours burn time
32,850 divided by 16 =	_____ divided by 16 =
2,053 number of 16-hour days	_____ number of 16-hour days
2,053 divided by 365 days =	_____ divided by 365 days =
5.6 years with cigarette lit	_____ years with cigarette lit

We recognize that these calculations are not precise, but the basic logic is sound. These calculations mean that Tom had a cigarette lit, and ready for smoking, a total of 5.6 waking years. No matter how you count, this is an incredible amount of time devoted to one activity. How many years have you had a cigarette lit and ready for smoking during your lifetime? We would bet it probably exceeds any other single activity in your life. You have probably spent more time smoking than you have eating, taking a shower, driving to work, and a hundred other things that you do on a regular basis.

Our purpose here is NOT to make you feel guilty about being a smoker or to embarrass you about the number of cigarettes you have smoked. We are merely interested in helping you understand the extent to which smoking affects your life.

RECORDING YOUR SMOKING PATTERN: YOU ARE THE AUTHOR

The next step is recording every cigarette you smoke during a 2 week period. This is accomplished by your filling out the smoking pattern section at the end of this chapter; Figure 3.1, 3.2, and 3.3. This section contains space for recording your nicotine consumption over 14 days. We will point out two features of this section. First, at the top of each page is a line for the date. The reason is simple. This book will become your autobiography, describing how you took control over smoking cigarettes and became a permanent nonsmoker. Second, the pages for recording are by hour of the day (left-hand side of the page) and by days within a week (top of the page). Most people are awake about 16 hours a day, some a little longer. We have allowed a total of 24 hours a day to accommodate the smoking life-style of any smoker. Choose the hours that fit your waking hours.

WEEK 1. HOW TO QUALIFY

This book will become your constant companion over the next two weeks. It is designed to fit neatly into a purse or a pocket. If you really need to quit smoking, all we ask is that you carry this book with you and record every cigarette you smoke. You will be doing this for the first two weeks, the Qualification period.

All smokers are not alike. Some smoke more than others. Some smoke stronger cigarettes than others. Some smoke all the way down to the filter. Others light one, take several puffs, and then light another before finishing the first. Some smokers even find themselves with several lit cigarettes around the room at the same time.

The reason we want you to record every cigarette you smoke during the next two weeks is to determine YOUR smoking pattern. During this Qualification period, we want you to be very conscious of WHEN you smoke and HOW MUCH you smoke.

Two Rules:

1. Don't start to cut down on the number of cigarettes you smoke during this Qualification period. Smoke in your normal pattern.

You need to know how much nicotine your body expects as normal.

2. Record every cigarette as you smoke. It is absolutely essential that you carry the book with you at all times and record the cigarette when you smoke it, not later.

We want you to be aware of the pattern of your smoking.

RECORDING YOUR CIGARETTE CONSUMPTION: AN EXAMPLE.

Sandra smoked a pack and a half of cigarettes a day for 31 years. Obviously, there were some days when she smoked a few more, some days when she smoked a few less. Our research has demonstrated that smokers adjust their daily consumption of cigarettes, more often than not, by increasing rather than decreasing the number. The reason is that reducing the number smoked usually creates problems. Your brain has come to rely on you to feed it the minimum daily allowance of nicotine. If it doesn't get the minimum daily allowance, withdrawal symptoms appear. In order to avoid those withdrawal symptoms, you have become a creature of habit — you smoke the amount it takes, every day, day in and day out, no matter what the circumstances.

Sandra knew the problems that occur when the brain is deprived of a drug it has come to expect. She had experienced all the signs listed as withdrawal symptoms by the American Psychiatric Association in the Diagnostic and Statistical Manual (DSM-IIIR, 1987, p. 151):

1. **Craving for nicotine**

2. **Irritability, frustration, or anger**

3. **Anxiety**

4. **Difficulty concentrating**

5. **Restlessness**

6. **Decreased heart rate**

7. **Increased appetite or weight gain**

Sandra also knew from many years experience that, in order to avoid these symptoms, she had better feed her brain its nicotine, and the feeding had better be exactly on schedule. It is not unusual for smokers to smoke a cigarette every 30 minutes. If you are awake for 16 hours, that means 30 to 32 cigarettes a day. Therefore, if you smoke your first cigarette of the day at 7 AM, record it by making a hash mark in the square for 7 AM the first day of Qualification. If you smoke your second cigarette at 7:35 AM with your coffee and newspaper, put a mark in the square for the 7:30 AM time period. Take your book with you to the car. Many smokers light up a cigarette almost automatically as they put the key in the ignition. If this is your pattern, record a mark in the square for that time period. We want you to record every cigarette smoked during the entire two weeks of Qualification.

Toward the end of the first week of Qualification, two things will happen. First, you will probably be amazed at how regular your smoking habit is. Those with whom we work report that they smoke cigarettes throughout the day almost like clockwork. Their cigarette smoking has been thoroughly interwoven into every aspect of their lives. It is connected with eating, drinking, working, breaks, driving, and sex. About the only activity most smokers engage in on a regular basis, that is not connected with smoking, is sleeping. However, if you think about it for a moment — sleeping is the only time your body is deprived of nicotine. That is why that first cigarette of the day probably tastes so good. It is also why you inhale those first cigarettes of the day so deeply. Your brain needs that shot of nicotine to make up for being deprived all night. The second thing you will notice toward the end of week 1 of Qualification is how BORING it is to record every cigarette. You'll hate having to take out that pen. If this is the way you feel, all we can say is: "GREAT!". This is a sign of progress. Hang in there, you've got another week of recording before you complete qualifying yourself to begin the Cooper/Clayton Method.

Remember Two Rules As You Complete the First Week and Start the Second Week

1. Don't Get Impatient

The first step as described contains two weeks for a reason. We want you to recognize (a) the pattern by which you smoke; and, (b) the amount you smoke. Our experience conducting smoking-cessation programs has been that the more accurate the recording during this period, the higher the success rate of participants.

2. Keep Smoking According to Your Normal Pattern

After completing the second week, you will be ready to take the second step toward becoming a nonsmoker.

WEEK 2. GETTING READY TO BECOME A NONSMOKER

As previously stated, recording each and every cigarette you smoke during the first week gets terribly boring. We know that. However, being bored with smoking and painfully aware of your smoking pattern is one way you can increase your resolve to become a nonsmoker. It is one thing to say, "I need to become a nonsmoker." It is quite another thing to become a nonsmoker. Following this program exactly as it is laid out will significantly improve your chances to go from the ORIGIN (smoking) to the DESTINATION (being a nonsmoker).

During this second week of Qualification, you will continue to record each and every cigarette you smoke. Keep your autobiographical book with you at all times. Recording the cigarettes you smoke will become almost as habitual as smoking itself. The first part of this second week will pass quickly. However, toward the end of the second week of Qualification, those with whom we have worked report that several things will happen.

First, you will begin to get anxious. Don't worry, this is a normal reaction. If you have smoked a long time, you probably have been with cigarettes longer than you've been married or worked in your job. Giving up cigarettes will be like giving up a very old and dear friend. Cigarettes have been used by you as a reward. You finish a difficult job and what do you do? You reward yourself with a cigarette. You finish a great meal and what do you do? You light up a cigarette. You wake up during the night and what do you do? You take out a cigarette, light up, and take a deep puff.

Second, you will begin to ask: "Do I really want to become a nonsmoker?" ONLY YOU CAN ANSWER THIS QUESTION. If, at the end of the second week of Qualification, you decide you are not ready — don't feel guilty about it. Perhaps the time is not right for you. Perhaps you are more addicted to nicotine than you realized. Perhaps what

37

appeared to you two weeks ago to be impelling reasons to become a nonsmoker, are not quite so impelling now. You CHOOSE to start smoking — you are the only person who can CHOOSE to become a nonsmoker.

Third, on the last day of the second week of Qualification, you will probably stay up later than usual. You may smoke more than you would normally smoke. You realize the die is cast. You will start on your journey to becoming a permanent nonsmoker tomorrow morning. You have made the commitment. You can do it. It will not be a "piece of cake," but it will be far easier than you think.

LOOKING AHEAD ...

You have now completed the two-week Qualification period. Congratulations! Your commitment to become a nonsmoker must be strong. We have found that a high percentage of those who have made such a commitment are successful. You have qualified yourself to start the Cooper/Clayton Method and begin your journey. It is not a long journey, particularly when compared with the length of time you have been smoking.

Remember, it is normal to be anxious at this time. If you have tried to become a nonsmoker on previous occasions, don't let a prior failure bog you down now. This is a new beginning for you.

The key to success with this Method is realizing that during STEP 2 — Substitution and Maintenance I, your body will be receiving enough nicotine to keep your brain satisfied. The brain can become accustomed to receiving its nicotine in a steady, timed-release fashion rather than as a "hit" seven seconds after inhaling the smoke (David P.L. Sachs, Current Pulmonology, 1990).

Don't try to focus on the destination of this journey. Take every day as it comes — concentrate on today, the next hour, or NOW — the future will arrive soon enough.

REVIEW OF QUALIFICATION FOR
THE COOPER/CLAYTON METHOD

Examination of your smoking patterns may have surprised you. A few of our patients thought they smoked more; most, however, were shocked at how many they smoked (especially during the second week, when it dawned on them they had only seven days left as a smoker).

Most of them, however, only received confirmation of what they had long suspected. Cigarettes had ceased to be a "casual" part of their lives. They found that they smoked in a highly structured manner. They were also surprised to note their total consumption of cigarettes varied little from day to day. Many of them qualified as "heavy" smokers (25 or more per day).

Perhaps the Cooper/Clayton Method to Become a Non-smoker, which was developed for heavy smokers, will be the answer you have sought to help you take control of your life again.

GOOD LUCK!

The Cooper/Clayton Method to Stop Smoking

Your Personal Diary and 24-Week Record of Your Victory Over Nicotine

_____

Your Name

_____

Date

YOUR PERSONAL DIARY

DATE		SUN	MON	TUE	WED	THU	FRI	SAT
AM	6:00							
	6:30							
	7:00							
	7:30							
	8:00							
	8:30							
	9:00							
	9:30							
	10:00							
	10:30							
	11:00							
	11:30							
	12:00							
PM	12:30							
	1:00							
	1:30							
	2:00							
	2:30							
	3:00							
	3:30							
	4:00							
	4:30							
	5:00							
	5:30							
	6:00							
	6:30							
	7:00							
	7:30							
	8:00							
	8:30							
	9:00							
	9:30							
	10:00							
	10:30							
	11:00							
	11:30							
	12:00							
AM	12:30							
	1:00							
	1:30							
	2:00							
	2:30							
	3:00							
	3:30							
	4:00							
	4:30							
	5:00							
	5:30							
TOTALS:								

You chose to start smoking, you can now choose to stop!

41   Figure 3-2

YOUR PERSONAL DIARY

	DATE	SUN	MON	TUE	WED	THU	FRI	SAT
AM	6:00							
	6:30							
	7:00							
	7:30							
	8:00							
	8:30							
	9:00							
	9:30							
	10:00							
	10:30							
	11:00							
	11:30							
	12:00							
PM	12:30							
	1:00							
	1:30							
	2:00							
	2:30							
	3:00							
	3:30							
	4:00							
	4:30							
	5:00							
	5:30							
	6:00							
	6:30							
	7:00							
	7:30							
	8:00							
	8:30							
	9:00							
	9:30							
	10:00							
	10:30							
	11:00							
	11:30							
	12:00							
AM	12:30							
	1:00							
	1:30							
	2:00							
	2:30							
	3:00							
	3:30							
	4:00							
	4:30							
	5:00							
	5:30							
TOTALS:								

You chose to start smoking, you can now choose to stop!

Figure 3-3   42

CHAPTER 4

STEP 2. REPLACEMENT THERAPY AND MAINTENANCE I

In Chapter 3, you began writing an autobiographical account of your life as a smoker. After recording every cigarette you smoked for two weeks, you know how important smoking is to you. By now, you are probably bored to death with the "process" of smoking. Almost everyone who decides to use the Cooper/Clayton Method picks up this book and is all fired up to become a nonsmoker RIGHT NOW.

Our research indicates that, at this point, the initial decision to become a nonsmoker may be an emotional one. We have found that, as smokers record their smoking patterns for two weeks of Qualification, their emotional decisions become more objective. This occurs as they realize they are not casual smokers. If you are like the hundreds of smokers we have worked with, you were probably surprised to see how patterned, how regimented, your smoking really is. Regardless, you will at least realize the pattern in which you provide your brain with nicotine.

The Qualification period constituted the "origin" of the journey to your "destination" as a nonsmoker. During Qualification, you identified your starting point with great precision. We are pleased you followed our plan and recorded your smoking patterns for two weeks. NOW YOU REALIZE WHAT A SIGNIFICANT ROLE CIGARETTE SMOKING PLAYS IN YOUR LIFE.

The next step of the program will probably produce greater anxiety for you. That is normal. We tend to experience anxiety when we are uncertain about the outcome of some event. Let us start to reduce your anxiety by telling you what this step is NOT. We will then assist you to further reduce your level of anxiety by telling you what this step IS.

WHAT REPLACEMENT THERAPY IS NOT

Replacement therapy is NOT COLD TURKEY! If you ever tried to become a nonsmoker by going cold turkey, you know that this approach is not always satisfactory. If it were, you probably wouldn't be reading this book. It may be too abrupt. Let's review the physical withdrawal symptoms described in Chapter 3. Some or all of these may occur when you suddenly deny the brain nicotine after an extended use of tobacco products. As you will recall, the physical symptoms can include:

(1) Craving for nicotine

(2) Irritability, frustration, or anger

(3) Anxiety

(4) Difficulty concentrating

(5) Restlessness

(6) Decreased heart rate

(7) Increased appetite or weight gain

We predict you experienced some or all of these when you previously attempted to suddenly drop your nicotine intake to zero. You will not abruptly stop using nicotine in this program. You will use a product that contains the same nicotine provided by cigarettes. The product is Nicoderm® (nicotine transdermal system). A little later in this chapter we will tell you exactly how to use this alternate source of nicotine.

You will first win your battle with cigarettes. You will become a nonsmoker but you will continue to give your brain the nicotine it wants. You will notice something very interesting during this period. Your brain is not discriminating. It could care less how you feed it nicotine, as long as it gets the AMOUNT it wants and WHEN it wants it. The Nicoderm® (nicotine transdermal system) is designed to give you nicotine throughout the 24 hours of a day. The Nicoderm® (nicotine transdermal system) is packaged in 3 different strengths: 21 mg, 14 mg, and 7 mg. Your physician or dentist can help you determine the strength of Nicoderm® (nicotine transdermal system) that is right for you, based on the amount of nicotine you formerly received from cigarettes, your weight, your overall health, history of cardiovascular disease, and other medical factors.

You will use NO CIGARETTES from this day forward. You will not stop using nicotine right away; you will stop using cigarettes to get your nicotine.

Now, go back and review your smoking habits as recorded in the 2 week Qualification Period. If you follow the pattern established by most of those with whom we have worked, you will probably fall into one of two groups. You will be either a SITUATIONAL SMOKER or a REGI-MENTED SMOKER. In either instance, you and your physician or dentist can custom design the Cooper/Clayton Method to meet your needs.

THE SITUATIONAL SMOKER

This individual smokes in a manner different from the patterns exhibited by a large majority of smokers (i.e., those who smoke every day throughout the day). Sharon was such a smoker. She did not smoke at all from the time she got up in the morning until she had completed dinner that evening. Typically, she started smoking after dinner and consumed 10 to 20 cigarettes that evening, starting with the after-dinner cigarette and ending with the last cigarette before bedtime. She discovered that her pattern from the 2 week Qualification period was closer to 20 cigarettes on most days. Her physician or dentist will help her to choose the appropriate strength nicotine dosage.

Another SITUATIONAL SMOKER, Barbara, smoked 30 cigarettes each day during working hours, Monday through Friday. She never smoked at home, where she wanted to be a good role model for her young son. On weekends, she often volunteered to run errands for her neighbors. While doing so, she could sneak a cigarette or two. Because her most common pattern was that of a heavy smoker, Barbara would probably be advised by her physician or dentist to start on the 21 mg Nicoderm® (nicotine transdermal system) and use it daily, even on weekends, for 6 to 8 weeks. Then her dosage will be adjusted by prescribing a lower nicotine content patch.

John smoked only at parties or other social occasions. He smoked particularly heavily when consuming alcohol. It was not unusual for him to go one or more weeks without cigarettes. Once he started smoking, it was not unusual for him to smoke an entire pack during an extended evening of cocktails, conversation, and dinner with friends. Because John's smoking pattern is so episodic, so erratic, it is likely he is not addicted to nicotine, at least not in a physiological sense. In our opinion, it would be inappropriate for John to be using a nicotine patch to "become a nonsmoker." His physician or dentist who counsels with John about his smoking will make this final decision about the use of Nicoderm® (nicotine transdermal system).

WHAT DO THESE SITUATIONAL SMOKERS HAVE IN COMMON? First, it can be predicted that they will score "low" to "moderate" on scales designed to measure dependence on nicotine, such as the Fagerstrom scale found in Chapter 3. Second, their total consumption of cigarettes during any given day would be relatively low. Third, each of the SITUATIONAL SMOKERS described above is accustomed to going for long periods of time without using nicotine. Their schedule for use of nicotine would probably not begin to meet the needs of a heavy smoker. It is important for such smokers to get enough replacement nicotine to satisfy their needs, but not too much.

THE REGIMENTED SMOKER

This person smokes in a more structured pattern as the smoking record during Qualification will show. Typically, this individual will score in the "high" range on Fagerstrom's scale of nicotine dependence. The most "frequent" smoking pattern we have observed for the REGIMENTED SMOKER is 1 cigarette each 30 minutes. Since the typical person is awake for 16 hours, and usually spends 3 time periods each day eating, they usually smoke 2 cigarettes each hour during the 15 hours they smoke. Thus, they consume 30 cigarettes, plus or minus 2, each day. For the REGIMENTED SMOKER, smoking is patterned rather than erratic or casual. Our clinical experience with hundreds of REGIMENTED SMOKERS shows they need a steady dose of nicotine to match the pattern of nicotine consumption they received from cigarettes.

Some regimented smokers may not smoke large numbers of cigarettes. Mary only smoked 8 cigarettes a day, day in and day out. She had two early in the morning, one when she had breakfast and one on the way to work. Then, at breaktime, she would have another and a fourth one at lunch. The fifth cigarette was smoked at about 3 in the afternoon, the 6th on the way home from work. The 7th cigarette was smoked during the news hour, right after dinner. The last cigarette was smoked immediately prior to getting ready for bed. Mary was as regular as clock work, but did not consume many cigarettes during the day. Mary was an organized and disciplined person. She will receive counseling from her physician or dentist about the correct strength dosage.

Upon review of your own record, you and your physician or dentist can custom design your program to meet your particular nicotine needs. We will describe a typical program for each of the two most common patterns.

NICODERM® (nicotine transdermal system): NICOTINE REPLACEMENT THERAPY

The nicotine in Nicoderm is the same nicotine you have been getting from cigarettes. However, you get nicotine into the blood system without also breathing in the thousands of gasses contained in cigarette smoke. There are several things you need to understand about Nicoderm and how to use it.

Nicoderm is a Transdermal Nicotine Delivery System

Patches that deliver a drug are not an entirely new phenomenon. You may have worn a patch to take care of motion sickness or, if you are female, to deliver estrogen.

The patch allows the drug to enter the skin (transdermal or "across the skin") and then to flow into the bloodstream which delivers it to the brain receptor sites that are poised to measure the amount of nicotine in the blood.

Nicoderm® (nicotine transdermal system) Provides a Steady Dose of Nicotine

The nicotine patch provides a steady release of nicotine. You should know from the outset that it does not provide a nicotine hit like a cigarette. Within 7 seconds after you take a puff from a cigarette, there is measurable nicotine in the brain. Nicoderm provides nicotine in a more controlled fashion. Therefore, there is no quick hit, like with a cigarette.

Nicoderm Provides An Adequate Amount of Nicotine

The patches are designed to deliver the amount of nicotine indicated by the 21 mg, 14 mg, and 7 mg strengths. The average plasma nicotine concentration is 17 nanograms per milliliter of blood for people wearing the 21 mg patch. This is great for even heavy smokers. The body's thermostat for nicotine, the "nicostat," is set at generally about 18 nanograms per milliliter (David P.L. Sachs, Current Pulmonology, 1987). This means that most heavy smokers will be comfortable with a 21 mg patch. There may be some slight withdrawal symptoms, but the Nicoderm patch usually delivers enough nicotine to satisfy — to keep the smoker from reaching for a cigarette.

Remember:

As with any medication, there are risks and side effects associated with use. (The most frequent side effects include skin irritation, headache, and sleep disturbances.) Please refer to the "Special Considerations for Nicoderm® (nicotine transdermal system) Use" at the beginning of this book, as well as patient instructions located in the back of the book.

As you smoked cigarettes over a period of years, you increased the number of cigarettes, and the nicotine, you provided the brain. The brain became "comfortable" at the higher level. It will also become comfortable with the level of nicotine provided by the nicotine patch, and will accept the new reduced level as normal after only a few days.

How Long Does It Take for Nicoderm to Work?
As soon as the patch is applied, the nicotine in the patch begins to make the journey from the patch, through the rate controlling membrane, toward

the blood stream. Therefore, within a short time after applying the patch, nicotine is already in the blood. However, you should know that the time to "peak" blood nicotine levels takes from two to about four hours. Does that mean that you will be climbing the walls? Not necessarily! For a heavy smoker still smoking cigarettes, it usually takes anywhere from one to three hours before peak blood nicotine levels are reached. If you are a heavy smoker you know this. You may wake up early in the morning and smoke a number of cigarettes close together in order to get comfortable.

Nicoderm Delivers Nicotine 24 hours a Day

Nicoderm is designed to provide a steady dose of nicotine over a 24 hour period. You have been used to smoking only during the time you are awake. Nicoderm keeps on working, even while you are asleep. It means that, after your first day on the patch, you will be waking up with some blood nicotine. When you were smoking, the reason you reached for a cigarette immediately upon waking, was because you were nicotine deficient after a night of nonsmoking. One problem encountered by patients using the nicotine patch is "vivid dreams" and some sleep disturbances. These generally disappear in a few weeks at the most.

Important Aspects of Applying Nicoderm

Step 1.   Choose a non-hairy, clean, dry area of your front or back above the waist or the upper outer part of your arm. Do not put Nicoderm patches on skin that is burned, broken out, cut, or irritated in any way.

Step 2.   Do not remove the Nicoderm patch from its sealed protective pouch until you are ready to use it. Nicoderm patches will lose nicotine to the air if you store them out of the pouch. Before putting on the patch, tear open the pouch. Do not use scissors to open the pouch because you might accidentally cut the patch. Discard the used patch you take off by putting it in the pouch that you take the new patch out of. The used patch should be thrown away in the trash out of reach of children and pets (see Step 7).

Step 3.   A stiff, clear, protective liner covers the sticky silver side of the Nicoderm patch —the side that will be put on your skin. The liner has a slit down the middle to help you remove it from the patch. With the silver side facing you, pull one half of the liner away from the Nicoderm® (nicotine transdermal system) patch starting at the middle slit. Hold the Nicoderm patch at one of the outside edges (touch the sticky side as little as possible), and pull off the other half of the protective liner. Throw away this liner.

Step 4. Immediately apply the sticky side of the Nicoderm patch to your skin. Press the patch firmly on your skin with the palm of your hand for about 10 seconds. Make sure it sticks well to your skin, especially around the edges.

Step 5. Wash your hands when you have finished applying Nicoderm. Nicotine on your hands could get into your eyes and nose and could cause stinging, redness, or more serious problems.

Step 6. After approximately 24 hours, remove the patch you have been wearing. Choose a "different" place on your skin to apply the next Nicoderm patch and repeat Steps 1 to 5. Do not return to a previously used skin site for at least one week. Do not leave on the Nicoderm patch for more than 24 hours because it may irritate your skin and because it also loses strength after 24 hours.

Step 7. Fold the used Nicoderm patch in half with the silver side together. After you have put on a new patch, take its pouch and place the used folded Nicoderm patch inside of it. Throw the pouch in the trash away from children and pets.

You may notice a slight itching shortly after you apply the patch each day and the skin around the patch may turn slightly red. This will not occur for everyone. If it occurs for you, be patient. This should not last very long. It is a localized irritation related primarily to the nicotine crossing the skin barrier. It is temporary. If it does continue contact your prescribing doctor or dentist for advice.

When to Apply Nicoderm

We recommend that you pick a time and establish a ritual of changing the patch at that time every day. Perhaps the best schedule is to change and apply the new patch first thing in the morning. Most of us are used to starting a new day with all of the important rituals. Smokers were used to getting a new start on nicotine consumption first thing in the morning. Therefore, at the beginning of your waking day is probably the best time to begin this new way of giving your brain nicotine for the next few weeks.

What Time of the Week to Start on Nicoderm

There are credible arguments for both sides of this one. Some would argue that your best bet is a weekend or a vacation, when you are relaxed and under less stress. On the basis of our 7 and one-half years of clinical experience with groups of people using nicotine replacement therapy, we recommend that the best time to start becoming a nonsmoker is during the work week, preferably on a Monday. Your smoking was probably most regimented and patterned during working hours. This is the best time to deal with not smoking. It is also the time your brain is occupied and your thoughts about cigarettes are suppressed by work related activities. Remember, you will still be getting nicotine in amounts large enough to minimize withdrawal symptoms. At this stage, you have only changed your source of nicotine from the cigarettes to Nicoderm.

How Long Should One Use Nicoderm?

The use of Nicoderm systems for longer than three months has not been studied. Therefore, no solid data exist concerning the effectiveness of the Nicoderm patch if used longer than 12 weeks. The instructions for Nicoderm recommend one approach to be a period of 6-8 weeks on the 21 mg patch, 2-4 weeks on the 14 mg patch, and 2-4 weeks on the 7 mg patch; a total of 10-16 weeks. As you know by now, our goal in the Cooper/ Clayton Method is to break completely your dependence on nicotine. We therefore urge you to set specific goals for making the transition from one patch to the next lowest dosage patch and to follow the pattern recommended by your doctor or dentist.

PATTERNS OF NICODERM®
(nicotine transdermal system) USE
FOR SITUATIONAL SMOKERS

The SITUATIONAL SMOKER has trained the brain receptor sites to be patient. During the time these individuals do not smoke, their receptor sites have been trained not to expect a steady supply of nicotine. In the Cooper/Clayton Method, each of the situational smokers will use a starting dose of Nicoderm consistent with the total amount of nicotine they previously gave themselves daily from cigarettes. This is the replacement part of the "nicotine replacement" therapy. Your physician or dentist may choose to adjust your starting dose if you have cardiovascular disease or weigh less than 100 pounds. Each of the situational smokers was using nicotine as a "reward." The steady dose of nicotine into their bloodstream from Nicoderm will remove the "reward" aspect of smoking. This should make it easier for these individuals to become nonsmokers.

Sharon was able to go the entire work day without smoking. However, every night, she would smoke between 10 and 20 cigarettes. Her physician or dentist can advise her about the most appropriate nicotine transdermal patch dosage to meet her nicotine needs. The nicotine from the patch should replace what she was getting from her somewhat erratic pattern of smoking.

Barbara, on the other hand, smoked heavily during working hours and very little during evenings or weekends while at home with her son. Because of her high average daily consumption, 30 cigarettes, Barbara probably has high nicotine needs. Her prescribing doctor or dentist will individualize her starting dose and advise her as to how to use the Nicoderm patch.

John, as you will recall, is only an occasional user of cigarettes. It can be predicted his dependence on nicotine is extremely low. In our opinion, it would be inappropriate for John to begin using Nicoderm.

In NO INSTANCE should either Sharon or Barbara, nor any other SITUATIONAL SMOKER, start with a higher dose of Nicoderm than is indicated by their doctor or dentist, who may base his/her recommendation on their smoking pattern. Neither should they use cigarettes and Nicoderm interchangeably. They should STOP SMOKING cigarettes at the end of the Qualification Period and substitute Nicoderm as their only source of nicotine for the remainder of the program.

PATTERNS OF NICODERM
USE FOR REGIMENTED SMOKERS

The instructions for use of Nicoderm suggest a starting dose of the 21 mg patch for the individual who smokes more than 1/2 pack of cigarettes per day, weighs 100 pounds or more, and has no history of cardiovascular disease. The suggested starting dose for the individual who smokes less than 1/2 pack per day, weighs less than 100 pounds, or has a history of cardiovascular disease, is the 14 mg patch.

Mary was our very disciplined smoker — 8 a day, never any more and never any less. Mary's starting dose of Nicoderm will be determined by her prescribing doctor or dentist. It is possible someone like Mary, who doesn't smoke a lot of cigarettes daily, but who has them spaced out evenly, may be a very efficient smoker.

Joan was a REGIMENTED SMOKER. She smoked one cigarette every 30 minutes, day in and day out. While on an automobile trip, she could almost tell how long she had been driving that day by counting the cigarettes she had smoked — one every half hour. During a normal day, when she worked as an account manager at a brokerage firm, she was a very patterned smoker — 30 cigarettes per day — every day — sick or well. A copy of Joan's smoking record is shown in Figure 4.1.

A review of her smoking patterns during the Qualification period indicates that she is not a casual user of nicotine. Her brain receptor sites have been trained, probably since Joan was a teenager, to expect 10 small doses of nicotine (one from each puff) every 30 minutes, every waking hour of the day. Joan's nicotine replacement pattern should be correct for Joan. It may not be correct for Sharon, Barbara, or John, nor would their pattern of nicotine consumption necessarily meet Joan's nicotine needs.

Joan smoked a cigarette each 30 minutes. By the way, this is a very common pattern. In our studies, approximately 65% to 70% of heavy smokers fit the 30-per-day pattern. Our research also shows that, regardless of cigarette brand, the brain receptor sites of the 30-per-day smoker have been trained to expect "some" nicotine every 30 minutes. Many patients report that the quantity is not as critical as the regularity, as long as some nicotine is provided to their brain every 30 minutes. Joan stopped smoking cigarettes at the end of the Qualification period. She continued to provide nicotine to her brain, but used only the alternate source of nicotine, Nicoderm® (nicotine transdermal system), the 21 mg patch strength.

Regardless of your previous smoking pattern, whether you are a situational or a regimented smoker, we will describe the Substitution process in detail. We realize it is not easy for you to become a nonsmoker. In most cases, you have been smoking over a number of years. Making it through Replacement Therapy will assist with relief of nicotine withdrawal symptoms.

WHAT REPLACEMENT THERAPY IS

REPLACEMENT THERAPY IS A TEMPORARY ALTERNATE WAY TO GIVE YOUR BRAIN THE NICOTINE IT CRAVES. For the moment, you may want to consider two basic points.

1. During Replacement Therapy, your brain will not be deprived of nicotine. The nicotine you will get from the alternate source should be enough to satisfy your brain and help relieve the craving that is experienced with withdrawal.

2. Later, we will tell you how to very gently wean yourself from the alternate source. But for now, let's concentrate on the immediate issue — eliminating your use of cigarettes.

During the Replacement Therapy step, all you are actually doing is teaching your brain to accept an altered dosage route for the nicotine it craves while you participate in a comprehensive behavioral smoking-cessation program.

MAINTENANCE I: ON THE ROAD TO SUCCESS

HOUR 1 —THE FIRST DAY

This is where the rubber meets the road. Today you take control of your smoking and begin the process of breaking your addiction to nicotine. Today, TODAY, you will not be smoking. Instead, you will be getting your nicotine in an alternate form. You have recorded all of those cigarettes you smoked during the Qualification step of the program, probably a very boring exercise. Now we begin.

****

Since our research shows that a significant percentage of smokers are regimented smokers, we will describe the manner in which Joan, one of the regimented smokers who participated in the Cooper/Clayton program, found to be the most effective way to use Nicoderm to meet her "needs."

****

Joan, as well as other regimented smokers who have succeeded with the Cooper/Clayton Method, agreed that Replacement Therapy and Dose Maintenance I is a significant change from smoking. They also agree that the weekly support group meetings helped make this step manageable. Support groups are an integral part of the Cooper/Clayton Method, a comprehensive behavioral smoking-cessation program. This is the period we call Replacement Therapy and Maintenance I. For 6 weeks, she got the nicotine she needed only from Nicoderm. The amount of nicotine she received was not as much as she had been getting from cigarettes, but it was sufficient to satisfy her craving for cigarettes.

We encourage persons using the Cooper/Clayton Method to concentrate on getting through each hour of the first day, and then each day of the next 6 to 8 weeks. Therefore we will follow Joan, one of hundreds of successful users of the Cooper/Clayton Method, through her first day of the Substitution and Maintenance I step.

JOAN'S STORY
(AND THAT OF MANY, MANY OTHERS)

Joan normally got up at 6 AM. She usually smoked her first cigarette of the day before showering. Today, instead of smoking, she would receive all of her nicotine from Nicoderm® (nicotine transdermal system). To make it easier, she had "flushed" her remaining cigarettes at bedtime the previous night. She wanted to give herself every opportunity to succeed.

As soon as the alarm awakened her, Joan's felt her fear level rising. She found herself looking at the 21 mg Nicoderm patch and saying: "Do I really want to give up my old trusted friend for that silly looking little thing? I must be crazy." You know exactly how she felt, don't you? She wasn't crazy and neither are you. You both are just ready to begin the process of becoming nonsmokers.

She then jumped out of bed and headed for the shower. Immediately prior to getting in the shower, she put Nicoderm on her upper left arm. This morning, she decided to stay in the shower longer than normal just to get things in perspective — to talk to herself about the challenge she was facing and her commitment to becoming a nonsmoker. As she was drying off, Joan felt the tingling and itching feeling on her arm. She knew that this was "normal" and that the tingling would probably be gone soon. It occurred to her, this little patch on her arm would be providing her with nicotine, the same nicotine in her cigarettes. Dr. Cooper had told her that it would take 2 to 4 hours before the level of nicotine reached a peak. She felt confident nicotine would soon be making its way to the brain. The Nicoderm patch would provide her nicotine all day.

Joan wondered briefly what she would do with her hands if she wasn't smoking and then thought: during every half hour of my waking day I have a lit cigarette in my hand only five minutes; for 25 minutes of every half hour I don't have a cigarette in my hand; now, for the total half hour, I'll just do what I do when I don't smoke. We have found that people becoming nonsmokers often increase their productivity. In fact, smokers usually take an additional 33 minutes a day beyond their free or break time, just for smoking rituals. Don't worry about what to do with your hands, our experience is that it is a much less significant problem than smokers realize. Our patients consistently report that the nicotine from the patch is adequate to prevent the restlessness and anxiety that caused hand wringing when they attempted to go cold turkey. Fumbling with your hands was a withdrawal sign. You are not in withdrawal now. You are getting nicotine from the Nicoderm patch. Reaching for the pocket or purse also goes away very rapidly.

****

REMEMBER:

Joan was a 30 cigarette-per-day smoker. She had smoked for 25 years. Her nicotine dependence score was in the "HIGH" dependence range. The 21 mg Nicoderm patch will not give her as much nicotine as the 30 cigarettes, but it would give her enough to be comfortable. The goal of the Cooper/Clayton Method is to start with a "reduction" in the amount of nicotine received daily. The body's monitor of nicotine concentrations in the blood, its nicostat, is usually set at about 18 nanograms per milliliter (ng/ml) of blood (a nanogram is one one-billionth of a gram or 1/1,000,000,000 gram). The steady-state blood nicotine level achieved with a 21 mg Nicoderm patch is about 17 ng/ml. Joan knew she would be able to get enough nicotine to be comfortable; not completely 100% comfortable, but close enough. Assuming she previously received about 1 mg of nicotine from each cigarette or 30 mg per day, the Nicoderm 21 mg patch results in approximately 70% replacement and should significantly reduce any withdrawal symptoms. She could accept that. She couldn't accept 0% She wouldn't have to.

****

MAINTENANCE I — Hour 2

Joan noted that the nicotine was doing its thing with her brain. Her brain was bound to be a little suspicious. It hadn't gotten that first big jolt of the morning that it was used to, but it was satisfied. It was receiving a steady dose of nicotine from Nicoderm. She knew she was on the upswing and that within a little while, she would reach the peak nicotine concentration.

Now Joan went through her normal routine. She normally took one hour to get dressed, fed, and ready for her day.

Joan's third cigarette of the day frequently occurred during the second waking hour as she drove to work. When Joan climbed into the car at 7 AM, she found it comforting to feel the patch on her left upper arm. There was a strong association of smoking while riding in the car. This association was almost as strong as the association with eating and smoking.

MAINTENANCE I — HOUR 3

By now, Joan was at work, and beginning to get a little scared. She knew the Nicoderm® (nicotine transdermal system) patch was releasing nicotine, but she wondered if it would release enough. She was at work and work was stressful. Joan pulled herself together and engaged in some self-talk. She calmed herself down enough to know that when you are experiencing stress, your nicostat moves higher, and it takes more nicotine to keep you comfortable. Therefore, it was essential that Joan reduce the stress. Her brain must work for her, not against her. She took about five deep breaths to relax herself.

It was 8 AM and Joan was ready for a cup of coffee. She dearly loved that first cup of coffee at work. However, she also knew that she would have to begin making an adjustment. For all of Joan's adult life, smoking a cigarette and having that first cup of coffee of the work day were closely connected — as tight as any two things can be. Joan knew that every time she had the first cup of coffee, it would remind her of smoking. Joan liked her coffee black with no sugar or sweetener. Today, she added some cream and one lump of sugar to give it a different taste, different enough so she wouldn't be reminded of smoking. Joan had been told at her support group meeting that caffeine is processed two and one-half times faster in a smoker than a nonsmoker according to research conducted by Dr. Neal Benowitz and his colleagues. Joan knew it would be necessary to adjust her caffeine consumption as she reduced her daily nicotine intake. She did a quick calculation. On a normal day, she would drink 6 cups of caffeinated coffee. If she had gone cold turkey, the caffeine would stay in her body longer and give her the same effect as approximately 15 cups of coffee. Therefore, from now on she would reduce her caffeine by pouring her coffee about half from the caffeinated container and half from the de-caffeinated container.

Joan wanted to succeed. She desperately wanted to become a nonsmoker. She knew the easiest way to not achieve was to have a "pity party." She would resist the temptation this time. Giving up cigarettes and reducing her caffeine was something she was willing to do for herself. She was mature enough to accept a small amount of short-term discomfort in order to achieve the long-term improved quality of life she would experience as a nonsmoker.

MAINTENANCE I HOUR 4

By 9 AM, Joan was heavily involved in her work. Much of Joan's work involved using the telephone. Previously, when Joan received a telephone call, she would cradle the phone on her shoulder and light a cigarette. It was mechanical. This day, she was not smoking. She had made it a point, before leaving her desk yesterday, to toss all the cigarettes in her desk into the waste basket. They would be gone by this morning she knew. She did the same thing at home last night. The first thing she did in her office today was to move the telephone to the other side of the desk. It was going to be uncomfortable, but she was determined to answer the phone with her left hand instead of her right. Furthermore, she had made a commitment to talk on the phone only if she was standing. She knew one of her weaknesses was spending too much time on the phone. Standing up and using her left hand would break the association and help her with her time management skills.

The long time association bond that existed between talking on the telephone and smoking would go away much faster than she would expect. However, by 9:30 Joan knew, she really KNEW Nicoderm was working. She could feel the nicotine working because she wasn't craving a cigarette. This patch was really working!

WARNING:

If Joan found herself craving, really craving nicotine, having almost overpowering thoughts about smoking, this could mean she was not getting enough nicotine. However, we should not forget that smoking is related to psychological and social factors as well. On the physical addiction side, Joan might be expected to experience thoughts about cigarettes for a few days, but this would pass rapidly because she was getting nicotine in sufficient amounts to keep her reasonably comfortable.

MAINTENANCE I — HOUR 5

Joan was making tremendous progress. Her brain was accepting absorption of nicotine through the skin as a reasonable dosage route. While not as rapid a route as inhaling, it provided adequate nicotine to prevent much of the pain she previously experienced when she denied herself cigarettes. By 10 AM Joan had already achieved the peak blood nicotine level she would achieve this first day. She knew in her brain that the patch was working. This was her first break at work when she had not smoked. It felt great!

MAINTENANCE I — HOUR 6

By now she had gotten into the flow of things. It was clear the Nicoderm® (nicotine transdermal system) 21 mg patch was delivering nicotine to her brain, and in sufficient quantity to ward off withdrawal symptoms. Her brain was accepting as "normal" the slow, timed-release of nicotine into the bloodstream instead of the peaks it got when she smoked.

Since Joan's wakeup time was around 6 AM, noon was a big milestone — she had gone all morning without smoking. How long has it been since you went through the entire morning without a cigarette and didn't suffer?

HELPFUL HINT TO JOAN:

Many smokers "rev up" their body about 30 minutes before lunch with a couple of quick cigarettes. This serves to reduce their appetite (nicotine is an appetite suppressor) and accelerate the body's "idling speed" (basic metabolic rate, Grunberg et. al, 1986). Two things can be helpful here.

1. A piece of fruit (an apple is especially helpful) 30 to 45 minutes before lunch will help to suppress her appetite.

2. Using the first half of her lunch period for a brisk walk, before she ate, will help to "rev up" Joan's metabolic rate. She will not only feel better, but will probably also eat less.

MAINTENANCE I — HOUR 7

For many smokers, the most difficult cigarettes to give up are those in the morning. The reason for that is simple. Your body has been deprived of nicotine for about 8 hours while you were asleep. As soon as you wake up, your brain starts hollering — "Hey! You neglected me during the night. It's time to take care of my needs. Let's find that cigarette and start the feeding process."

Joan made it through the morning. She now faced a new challenge; going through the afternoon without smoking. Smoking is something she had done in connection with finishing lunch for years. She took our advice and tried the fruit and the walk also. She then ate just before going back to work. Getting busy immediately after eating helped take her mind off the cigarette she formerly smoked at that time. Nicoderm was working just the way it was designed, giving Joan a steady dose of nicotine, enough to prevent her from craving cigarettes.

****

ANOTHER HELPFUL HINT:

Many participants following the Cooper/Clayton Method find that reducing the amount of food intake at meals, stopping short of a "full" feeling, makes elimination of the after meal cigarette much easier. It also prevents your substituting overeating for the smoking you formerly did.

****

MAINTENANCE I — HOUR 8

Joan was aware of the association between smoking cigarettes and certain other activities in which she participated. Eating and smoking is a strong and frequent association or pattern. She had successfully broken that association twice today — following breakfast and, now, following lunch. The battle was not over, but she had reached the half-way point still winning. She had now spent 8 hours of her first day getting nicotine from her Nicoderm® (nicotine transdermal system) patch.

MAINTENANCE I — HOUR 9

Nicotine is a remarkable drug. It can be used to either pick you up or settle you down. Joan usually needed a pick-me-up about this time of the day to take care of the early afternoon blahs. She engaged in a little self-talk about how effectively Nicoderm was working, actually beyond her wildest expectations. Then she remembered Drs. Cooper and Clayton saying that nicotine suppresses insulin output from the pancreas. This means that many smokers artificially raise blood sugar levels by smoking a cigarette or two and skipping a meal. When they give up nicotine, usually cold turkey, they feel like they are in first gear and can't get out. They feel like they have no energy. When Joan had tried to give up cigarettes before, she had started eating a candy bar every mid-afternoon. She now realized that she was not addicted to chocolate, but was instead treating transient lowered blood sugar. Although she was still getting nicotine from the Nicoderm patch, it made sense to Joan to get up from her desk and take a brisk walk. This would help her get over the afternoon blahs. She would use half of the five minutes she formerly spent "relaxing" with a cigarette. The nicotine from the cigarette actually was stimulating her. Her pulse rate would be increased several beats per minute. She felt more alert. Now, she would accomplish the same feeling of alertness with her brisk walk. An unhealthy behavior was replaced by a healthy behavior!

MAINTENANCE I — HOUR 10

Joan's 10th hour of this banner day came without much fanfare. She was pleased to note that, with adequate amounts of nicotine from Nicoderm, she was NOT craving cigarettes. This fact convinced Joan of two things: (1) Nicoderm is an aid for relief of nicotine withdrawal symptoms; and (2) it is nicotine she craved instead of cigarettes. The Nicoderm patch works. It provides the nicotine the brain needs.

MAINTENANCE I — HOUR 11

Joan got off work at 4:30. What a day! As she headed for the parking lot, she couldn't believe it. After hauling cigarettes to work all those years, today she made it through the entire workday with Nicoderm and NO CIGARETTES.

Before she started following the Cooper/Clayton Method, she had never gone through an entire workday without smoking. She experienced a very warm glow of success when she completed that first day at work without cigarettes. Another participant, Jeanie, worked in a university medical center. At the end of the work day, she went to the doctor she worked for and said: "I want you to give me a round of applause. Today is the first day in 30 years that I haven't smoked at work!" She had accomplished something. She had been victorious over the morning and had conquered the afternoon!

****

WARNING:

During the Substitution-Maintenance I portion of the Cooper/Clayton Method to Stop Smoking, Joan was not being deprived of nicotine. She was merely changing the way her body gets nicotine. It would have been easy at this point for Joan to get over-confident. She had to resist that temptation. Another temptation would be to deny her addiction and stop using the Nicoderm patch. That little voice inside her could have said: "Hey, you are taking control over cigarettes, and that is a big, BIG accomplishment. Why not take control over Nicoderm at the same time. Come on. You can take a short-cut and get off Nicoderm early." We have only one comment: "DON'T!" Resist that temptation. Those who have been most successful have followed the Cooper/Clayton Method precisely as it is written.

****

MAINTENANCE I — HOUR 12

By 5 PM Joan was home and ready to begin preparing for dinner. This is often a rough time for someone attempting to become a nonsmoker. Her normal routine had always been to kick off her shoes, heave a sigh of relief, and smoke a cigarette or two to decompress from the day's struggles and stress. Something else usually occurred at this time for Joan. She began to get that empty feeling about 45 minutes before dinner. She had always used cigarettes at that time to boost her metabolic rate and raise her blood sugar level. We had suggested to her that she eat an apple to achieve the same goal. Joan usually had dinner at 6 PM. Today, she ate an apple at 5:15. In addition to boosting the blood sugar level, eating an apple had the additional benefit of giving her some bulk in the stomach before starting her meal.

MAINTENANCE I — HOUR 13

Joan felt very good about her success to this point. She wanted to finish the day a winner. Certain things seem to fit perfectly together — peaches and cream, sugar and spice, the evening meal and cigarettes. So, immediately after her meal, we suggested she not just sit there. To do so would have reminded her of all those years she had an after dinner cigarette. Another thing Joan did was to alter the amount of food she ate. Persons using the Cooper/Clayton Method consistently report the following experience: "The more I ate, the more I craved that after-dinner cigarette." Joan noted that she could significantly reduce the desire to smoke after dinner if she followed one simple rule —"stop eating a little short of the full feeling." At 6:30, she brushed her teeth and took a stroll for 30 minutes. This is the meal she had dreaded most without cigarettes. She was amazed at how well the alternate source of nicotine was working.

MAINTENANCE I — HOUR 14

Joan made it through the dinner hour with no problems. When she smoked cigarettes, she remembered she used to feel a little saturated with nicotine at this point. This is normal. The metabolic half life of nicotine is 120 minutes, two hours. This means that two hours after 1 mg of nicotine is introduced into the body, one-half of it has been metabolized. Over the next two hours, half of the remaining one-half mg of nicotine is metabolized, and so on. Therefore, there is a slow build up of nicotine in the body of a smoker throughout the day.

Joan would no longer experience this feeling of saturation. Remember, she was attempting to keep the blood nicotine steady to prevent "craving" for nicotine. She remembered what a patterned smoker she was, and how she had kept her blood nicotine levels high with cigarettes. She was only changing her source of nicotine and the speed with which it reached the brain. She was still getting nicotine, but in a very steady flow. She was retraining her brain to accept this method of getting it's nicotine, rather than the 300 or so "hits" she formally gave it when she inhaled cigarette smoke all day long.

MAINTENANCE I — HOUR 15

Joan realized that today she was very conscious of not smoking. She had expected it to be somewhat difficult. She was pleasantly surprised however, that it had not been as difficult as she thought it would be. This was the time she began to feel the effect of following through on the commitment she had made to become a nonsmoker. She had gone almost an entire day without smoking. She was surprised at the ease with which she had accomplished this. The Nicoderm® (nicotine transdermal system) patch works!

MAINTENANCE I — HOUR 16

This was the last waking hour of Joan's day. As she was getting ready for bed, she felt a tremendous sense of accomplishment. She had gone a whole day without smoking. Furthermore, her brain had accepted rather easily a new way of getting nicotine. By using the Nicoderm patch, she had avoided all of the irritation of the burning process, and hadn't had carbon monoxide entering her lungs through the mainstream and the sidestream smoke. She was acutely aware of how good her mouth tasted. She spent an extra minute flossing and brushing her teeth. She was going to like this new life as a nonsmoker.

As Joan closed her eyes, she suddenly realized that she had gone an entire 24 hours, a whole day without smoking. Joan had felt dominated by cigarettes and smoking. Every time she had previously tried to give up smoking she felt miserable and deprived. Today was different. She knew she was getting nicotine through the skin and it seemed to satisfy her. It wasn't smoking, but she had made up her mind. This time she was taking control over one of the things in her life that she previously couldn't seem to control. She felt a sense of relief. If this was what she could expect without cigarettes, she could make it! For the first time in years, she had not smoked for a whole day and had not suffered physical withdrawal symptoms.

She touched the Nicoderm® (nicotine transdermal system) patch on her left shoulder and felt even more confident about the next day. Throughout the night, while Joan was asleep, the nicotine would be seeping through the skin and into her bloodstream. When Joan was smoking cigarettes, the steady infusion of nicotine into the bloodstream slowed when she went to bed. Tonight, she would continue to get some nicotine from the Nicoderm patch as she slept. This was important because during the years she smoked cigarettes, the nicotine from body tissues was slowly released into her blood as she slept. The Nicoderm patch would now provide small amounts of nicotine to her brain as she slept, possibly causing her to experience some sleep disturbances.

MAINTENANCE I: A SIX TO EIGHT WEEK PERIOD OF ADJUSTMENT

Joan made it through the first day without major problems. She was pleased. Tomorrow would be another day of nonsmoking. In fact, every day for the six to eight weeks of Maintenance I would involve Joan putting a 21 mg Nicoderm patch on immediately prior to her shower in the morning. Every day would bring another sense of victory and success, and a realization that she was conquering something that had previously controlled her. There would be days during this six to eight weeks when the stress and the years of association bonds with cigarettes would make her think she wanted a cigarette. Whenever this occurred, she had to remind herself that she no longer smoked. Although she was still a user of nicotine, cigarettes had ceased to be a part of her life. She continued to remind herself that cigarettes never solved a single problem for her. Every day she was getting adequate nicotine from Nicoderm to satisfy her physical dependence on nicotine.

She had been a patterned cigarette smoker and needed a steady supply of nicotine throughout the day. Even though she was receiving a reduced amount of nicotine, this alternate source continued to be adequate to prevent the physical withdrawal symptoms she faced previously when she attempted to eliminate cigarettes from her life.

Joan learned something else very important. Occasionally, her brain reminded her she needed more nicotine. Her former reaction had been to meet this need with a cigarette. Now, she had an option. She told her brain, "No way!, I am giving you nicotine from the Nicoderm patch, and only from the patch. Call me in 10 minutes." Often, the alternate nicotine source had her receptor sites comfortable before the 10 minutes was up.

****

SPECIAL NOTE

Joan remembered that Drs. Cooper and Clayton told her that some patients describe more vivid dreams during the first few weeks they wear the patch overnight, and that these dreams generally disappear in 4 or so weeks.

****

The use of cigarettes while wearing the nicotine transdermal patch could result in excessive nicotine blood levels. YOU SHOULD NOT SMOKE WHILE WEARING A NICOTINE TRANSDERMAL PATCH.

Occasionally participants report an almost overwhelming urge to "slip" a cigarette sometime during this 6-8 week period. They also report that, if they do slip, the cigarette didn't taste nearly as good as they expected. "Slipping" a cigarette only prolongs the inevitable — BEFORE YOU CAN BECOME A NONSMOKER YOU MUST TOTALLY ELIMINATE CIGARETTES AS A SOURCE OF NICOTINE.

Remember, your goal must be to limit your source of nicotine to the Nicoderm patch. The sooner you can put two consecutive weeks together with NO cigarettes, and get your nicotine ONLY from Nicoderm, the closer you move toward achieving your ultimate goal of zero nicotine.

Stated another way, the day you choose to limit your source of nicotine to Nicoderm only, you have taken a giant step. You must first free yourself from cigarettes. For some, this choice is made very early and no slips occur. For others, a slip or two delays this eventual decision. But remember, the only people who FAIL in their attempts to win their battle with cigarettes, are the ones who experience some difficulty and stop making an attempt.

The Cooper/Clayton Method is not magic, but it can help make the transition from smoker to nonsmoker manageable. The smoker who has chosen to become a nonsmoker has frequently tried and failed previously. The Cooper/Clayton Method is a behavioral smoking-cessation program to consider. It provides information on weight management, exercise, coping strategies, and other skills which can assist you to become a nonsmoker. The weekly support group meeting for 24 weeks is also helpful. Sharing experiences with others who share your goal of becoming a nonsmoker can help you maintain your resolve during times when you might be tempted to relapse. The combination of nicotine replacement therapy and support will increase your chances for success. You will also find the pleasure you receive from providing support to others very gratifying.

PLEASE REMEMBER ALSO, each unsuccessful "attempt" to stop smoking increases the likelihood the next attempt will result in success.

Joan was a heavy morning smoker, especially during the period between 9 and 11 AM. She had a tough time making it through this period the first day of Maintenance I, and had an even tougher time the second day. Part of Joan's problem was physical. The typical smoker receives 1 mg of nicotine from a cigarette. Joan's total nicotine intake with Nicoderm® (nicotine transdermal system) was reduced from those days when she had smoked 12 cigarettes between 6 and 11 AM. Her brain had been trained to expect 12 mg of nicotine during that period as normal. However, the amount of nicotine she received from Nicoderm was enough to keep her comfortable, if not totally satisfied.

A part of Joan's problem was psychological. This was a period of Joan's workday when pressure was most intense and she had always used cigarettes to help her survive the morning. This had become a deeply ingrained pattern of behavior, and she was especially fearful of going through that period without a crutch. Fortunately, the brain adjusts fairly rapidly to the lower level of nicotine. Joan noted that, by the end of the first week, the battle had become a mental rather than a physical problem, and she was winning the war. You also will note that, everyday you are away from cigarettes you will get stronger. We want you, just like Joan, to be a winner.

HELPFUL HINT:

Don't be disturbed if, during Maintenance II, you develop a cough for a few days. The cilia in the tracheobronchial tree are designed to sweep mucus toward the throat and clear out foreign matter. They were kept inactive during the day by your cigarette smoke. After you stop smoking, they function normally. Some individuals, who did not cough as smokers, report a cough some time during the first two to four weeks after they stop smoking cigarettes. This is no cause for alarm, and the cough should go away within three to four weeks. If not, check with your physician.

Also, a small percentage of ex-smokers develop mouth ulcers about this time. This occurs with or without use of an alternate nicotine product. If these lesions develop, they normally are of short duration, 10 to 14 days. They occur because the inner surface of the mouth is restoring itself, following the daily irritation of this tissue with hot cigarette smoke. The medical literature contains numerous articles about the increased incidence of apthous ulcers (mouth ulcers) following cessation of cigarette smoking. Many of these articles were written long before the development of Nicoderm, and most appeared years before any alternative nicotine products became available in the United States. If you experience mouth ulcers, just be patient. If the lesions persist, see your physician or dentist.

REVIEW

It took Joan two weeks to complete the Qualification step for entering the program. This two-week Qualification made her painfully aware of the degree to which her life was controlled by cigarette smoking, and the amount she smoked every day.

During the Replacement Therapy and Maintenance I steps of the program she had not given up nicotine, she had merely changed the way her brain got nicotine. This period has also moved her away from the mechanical habit of reaching for cigarettes. She wasn't home free yet, but was a LONG WAY from where she had been. She was no longer smoking cigarettes.

Her brain was getting enough nicotine to meet its needs. It had also come to accept the nicotine on a regular basis, rather than in short bursts, the way it received nicotine when she was a cigarette smoker.

Two questions Joan raised before she started the program had been answered. One, "What do I do with my hands?" As have hundreds of others, she found the answer — nothing. Joy, another program participant said about this: "When you no longer have a cigarette in your hands after you stop smoking, do the same thing with your hands you formerly did between cigarettes — nothing."

Second, Joan found that not having something in her mouth never became a problem. She realized that it is just not normal to hold a lighted object in your mouth that reaches 1600 degrees fahrenheit.

The most important thing to remember is that she was now not smoking. This was a major milestone in her life. Her goal was to continue adding a series of days just like this together so she would permanently be a nonsmoker.

****

ADDITIONAL INFORMATION ABOUT NICODERM® (nicotine transdermal system)

1. NICOTINE IS VERY SENSITIVE TO LIGHT AND HEAT.

Do not, repeat, do not leave a package of Nicoderm on the seat of your car, on the window ledge in your office, or in the trunk of your automobile. Do not carry the medication in a shirt pocket next to your body. Light and heat reduce the effectiveness of the nicotine.

Recommendation:

When you buy a box, take out only the patch you need each day. Put the rest in a cool, dark place. This will protect the medication from both light and heat.

2. A SPECIAL NOTE FOR WOMEN

The specific effects of Nicoderm treatment on fetal development are unknown. Therefore, pregnant smokers should first be encouraged to attempt to become nonsmokers using educational and behavioral modification approaches before using pharmacological approaches. Nicoderm should be used during pregnancy only if the likelihood of smoking cessation justifies the potential risk of use of nicotine replacement therapy by the patient who may continue to smoke. Your physician can assist you to make this decision.

An additional note is in order here. The nicotine needs of women may vary during certain phases of the menstrual cycle. Our experience has shown a significant number of women who have used the Cooper/Clayton Method report an increased need for nicotine during the PMS period. You may experience an increased craving for cigarettes during this time.

3. USE OF NICODERM AND OTHER DRUGS

As you follow the Cooper/Clayton Method, you first eliminate smoking cigarettes. You will then slowly reduce nicotine consumption, eventually eliminating nicotine totally from your life while participating in a comprehensive behavioral smoking-cessation program. It is important that you realize that smoking affects the way the body processes many other substances put into it. In addition, researchers have shown that smoking affects the body's metabolic rate. As you reduce the amount you smoke a number of changes, such as lowered metabolic rate and altered liver enzymes, may affect the way your body processes some drugs. Changes occur in the effectiveness of other drugs such as medicines prescribed for blood pressure, tranquilizers prescribed to alleviate anxiety or relax muscles, and other drugs designed to reduce pain. If you are taking other kinds of medication, we strongly urge you to consult with your physician or dentist. Tell your doctor that you are stopping the use of cigarettes and will also, in several weeks, be eliminating nicotine from your life. Ask if this might require some adjustment in the dosage of other prescribed medication. You may also want to consult with your pharmacist about the specific medication you are taking, and how it interacts with nicotine.

4. GENERAL PRECAUTIONS IN USING NICODERM®
(nicotine transdermal system)

A list of the precautions you should be aware of before using Nicoderm is provided in the instructions inside the box. These precautions should be referred to in case you have any questions about this product. Your physician, dentist, or pharmacist is also a source of specific information about this product.

5. BEHAVIOR MODIFICATION

The Patient Instructions for Nicoderm are quite clear — Nicoderm is a pharmacological agent which should be used as an adjunct to a comprehensive behavioral modification program. Smoking is a complex physical, cognitive, and affective or emotional behavior. The purpose of Nicoderm is to function as an aid to a comprehensive behavioral smoking-cessation program. It serves as a replacement for the nicotine formerly received from cigarettes. It can and does effectively relieve withdrawal symptoms. However, there are the other important aspects of smoking which require comprehensive behavioral modification.

Therefore, nicotine transdermal patches and other alternate forms of nicotine are to be used as adjuncts in smoking cessation. Cigarette smoking is a complex behavior, and becoming a nonsmoker involves much more than providing nicotine in a form other than the cigarettes. Cox and McKenna (1992) reviewed data from the clinical trials for nicotine transdermal patches. They reported that the success rate of those who have behavioral modification training plus the transdermal nicotine patch had twice the success rate of those who used the nicotine patch alone.

This book can be an aid to you in understanding how to make the transition from smoker to nonsmoker. The Cooper/Clayton Method is a comprehensive behavioral smoking-cessation program. Weekly support group meetings are an integral part of the program. A group of people with a similar problem and goal can provide significant support to each other during this difficult transition. Making a commitment to attend 24 support group meetings also adds an accountability element to your plan to become a nonsmoker. Smokers NEED this accountability to the group to increase their chances for success.

LOOKING AHEAD......

The next step in the Cooper/Clayton Method is based on the premise that eliminating nicotine from your life is a process, rather than a discrete event. It requires a lot of concentration and attention to detail. After 6 to 8 weeks on the 21 mg Nicoderm patch, Joan would begin the process of Elimination I and Maintenance II, by changing the strength of the Nicoderm to a 14 mg patch. This next phase of the Cooper/Clayton Method lasts 2 to 4 weeks and allows you to become accustomed to a reduction of nicotine. The 14 mg Nicoderm patch would be applied every day during this 2 to 4 week period.

Whether you were a situational smoker, like Sharon or Barbara, or a regimented smoker like Joan, you will find the Cooper/Clayton Method could work for you. It is a reasonable plan to make the transition from cigarettes to an alternate nicotine source. We hope you followed their lead, and now are using a nicotine replacement therapy product like Nicoderm as an aid to your comprehensive behavioral smoking-cessation program.

Now, sit back and contemplate your journey thus far. Aren't you proud of yourself? You should be. Regardless of whether you are a situational or a regimented smoker, you have eliminated cigarettes from your life. Nicotine is still being provided to your brain receptor sites. Our patients have consistently told us it may be easier to quit using alcohol and other mood altering drugs than it is to give up smoking cigarettes. Nicotine is an incredibly powerful dependence-producing drug.

****

YOU DID IT!

CONGRATULATIONS!

A VERY DIFFICULT PART OF THE JOURNEY IS BEHIND YOU!

JOAN'S RECORD — CIGARETTES

DATE		2/8	2/9	2/10	2/11	2/12	2/13	2/14
		SUN	MON	TUE	WED	THU	FRI	SAT
AM	6:00		I	I	I	I	I	
	6:30		I	I	I	I	I	
	7:00		I	I	I	I	I	
	7:30	I	I	I	I	II	I	I
	8:00	I	I	I	I	I	I	I
	8:30	I	I	I	I	I	I	I
	9:00	I	I	I	I	I	I	I
	9:30	I	I	I	I	I	I	I
	10:00	I	II	I	I	I	I	I
	10:30	I	I	I	I	I	I	I
	11:00	I	I	I	I	I	I	I
	11:30	I	I	I	I	I	I	I
	12:00	I	I	I	I	I	I	I
PM	12:30	I	I	I	I	I	I	I
	1:00	I	I	I	I	I	II	I
	1:30	I	I	I	I	I	I	I
	2:00	I	I	I	I	I	I	I
	2:30	I	I	I	I	I	I	I
	3:00	I	I	II	I	I	I	I
	3:30	I	I	I	I	I	I	I
	4:00	I	I	I	I	I	I	I
	4:30	I	I	I	I	I	I	I
	5:00	I	I	I	I	I	I	I
	5:30	I	I	I	I	I	I	I
	6:00	I	I	I	I	I	I	I
	6:30		I	I	I	I	I	I
	7:00	II	I	I	I	I	I	I
	7:30	I	I	I	I	I	I	I
	8:00	I	I	I	I	I	I	I
	8:30	I	I	I	I	I	I	I
	9:00	I	I	I	I		I	I
	9:30	I		I				I
	10:00	I						I
	10:30							
	11:00							
	11:30							
	12:00							
AM	12:30							
	1:00							
	1:30							
	2:00							
	2:30							
	3:00							
	3:30							
	4:00							
	4:30							
	5:00							
	5:30							
TOTALS:		30	32	33	31	31	32	30

Figure 4-1

CHAPTER 5

STEP 3. ELIMINATION I AND MAINTENANCE II

The past 6-8 weeks went by rapidly! Your recording of your smoking pattern plus your score on the Fagerstrom scale gave you valuable information. Once you established what your level of nicotine dependence was, you and your physician or dentist were able to custom structure a program to get you off cigarettes. You did this by providing your brain with an alternative source of nicotine.

You are probably surprised at how rapidly your brain accepted this new way of getting its' daily supply of nicotine. The Nicoderm® (nicotine transdermal system) patch is a relatively safe way to get nicotine. You should be pleased with your progress. You are now 6-8 weeks from your last cigarettes. Your body had to make more sudden adjustments during Nicotine Replacement and Dose Maintenance I than any other step in the Cooper/Clayton Method. You also learned some coping skills during this period from the comprehensive behavioral smoking-cessation program. You probably are feeling somewhat more positive about your prospects for remaining a nonsmoker.

The 6-8 week period of Substitution and Maintenance I was designed to allow your brain to adjust to three significant changes. The first change was substituting Nicoderm for cigarettes and becoming accustomed to the slow absorption of nicotine through the skin. The second change was learning to accept the sustained, steady absorption of nicotine to maintain blood levels. Finally, the third change was teaching your brain to accept the overall lower blood nicotine level as "normal."

You are also probably surprised to notice many of the association bonds with daily life events and cigarette smoking are becoming less intense. You originally trained your brain to associate smoking a cigarette with many of your daily activities. As an example, you poured a cup of coffee or a soft drink, lit a cigarette and inhaled, then sipped your drink. After repeating this sequence many times, a pattern of reinforcement occurred. When you poured the drink, you automatically thought of the cigarette. It requires some effort on your part to break this association, but it can be broken. You taught yourself to make the association between the coffee or soft drink and cigarette smoking. You can also teach yourself that these are no longer done together. Each time you repeat the first act without the second act, a new pattern of behavior is learned, and the old pattern, no longer reinforced, is soon forgotten.

Do you remember how, many times per day, you automatically reached for your pocket, purse, bedside table — all those places you formerly kept cigarettes? We predict that automatic reaching is almost gone in just 6-8 short weeks. In approximately 4-6 additional weeks, it will probably be totally gone. The reason is related to the law of positive reinforcement which states:

Any behavior which results in a positive state of affairs, or eliminates a negative state of affairs, or prevents development of a negative state of affairs, is positively reinforced and tends to become habit.

Your need for nicotine caused you to reach for cigarettes on a regular basis. Ten or so puffs on a cigarette and your need for nicotine ceased to exist, at least temporarily. From nicotine deficient to nicotine satiation in a very short period of time. Each time you craved nicotine you relieved the craving by reaching for a cigarette, lighting it, thus building your blood nicotine levels back up to your comfort zone.

The law of positive reinforcement means that the more rapidly a positive reaction follows the initial action, the easier it is to develop dependence on the initial act. You have begun the act of breaking your dependence on nicotine. You began when you stopped dosing yourself by inhaling a cigarette. You took a positive step toward your goal of becoming free from nicotine.

Recognizing the law of positive reinforcement is important. An acknowledged behavior is repeated, an ignored behavior is discarded. Each time you do not light the cigarette, the pattern weakens. In the same vein, we do not want to develop new association bonds between your daily events and Nicoderm® (nicotine transdermal system).

76

You are probably a little surprised to note how much confidence you have in Nicoderm. Putting the Nicoderm patch on is comforting. That proves two things. First, Nicoderm is an acceptable temporary aid to get your daily nicotine. Second, and more important, it is time to start backing off of Nicoderm.

Recall now how you got to your former 20, 30, 40, 50 or more per day cigarette habit — SLOWLY, VERY SLOWLY. Keeping that progression in mind is very important. You are now going to reduce your daily nicotine intake the same way — SLOWLY, VERY SLOWLY.

****

ATTENTION SITUATIONAL SMOKERS:

Remember, the ultimate goal of the Cooper/Clayton Method is to get you completely free of nicotine. There are as many variations of smoking patterns as there are situational smokers. Therefore, the principles that apply for the regimented smoker also apply to the situational smoker. The principles are these. First, you totally eliminate cigarettes as your source of nicotine. Second, you establish a comfort level with the alternate source of nicotine. The brain receptor sites adjust to two rather significant changes. One of these changes is the sustained release of nicotine from Nicoderm, as compared to the bolus effect when you were still smoking cigarettes. The other change is the amount of nicotine needed to achieve comfortable blood nicotine levels is reduced. It is during the Maintenance stage that these changes occur.

****

ELIMINATION I

Step 3 has two components. The first is Elimination I.

A high percentage of those who smoke are heavy smokers. As you recall, Joan formerly smoked 30 cigarettes a day. At this stage, she was using the 21 mg Nicoderm patch, 24 hours a day, and had been for six to eight weeks. Elimination I refers to switching to a lower dosage patch of Nicoderm: the 14 mg patch.

MAINTENANCE II — Sensing Victory

Joan found that during the first several days on the 14 mg Nicoderm® (nicotine transdermal system) patch, she was very much aware of the lower level of nicotine she was receiving. However, it was not nearly as bad as she thought it would be. Her brain very quickly accepted this reduced amount as "normal."

She had won a major battle. She had every right to be proud. So do you. Becoming a nonsmoker is not easy. It is one of the most difficult challenges some people ever face in life. Therefore, when you feel like celebrating, go ahead. You deserve it. Enjoy the feeling.

Just six or eight short weeks ago Joan was probably hoping, perhaps not really believing, that in such a short period of time she would be able to become a nonsmoker. The two weeks she recorded seemed to take forever. She was in a state of preparation. The six to eight weeks of the Replacement and Maintenance I phase must have looked like it would take a lifetime to complete. At times during that period, she probably thought: "Becoming a nonsmoker is the most difficult thing I have ever tried to do." She has now made the most difficult adjustment. Replacement and Maintenance are, by far, the most difficult parts of the entire program. Yet, virtually all of us believe in the principle of "No pain, no gain." There is something about having to struggle, to fight against the odds, to go head-to-head with adversity and win, that provides a sense of accomplishment.

The next step Joan had to take was making the switch from the 21 mg Nicoderm to the 14 mg patch (Elimination I). But this was more manageable than she thought it would be. Even so, it required discipline on her part. She knew she must be patient while her brain accepted this new level of nicotine as normal.

We have observed a very consistent pattern among participants at this stage. Though they questioned their ability to stop using cigarettes only 6-8 weeks ago, they now start looking far and wide for a smoker with whom they can share taking control of an addiction that previously controlled them.

CONTROLLED OR BEING IN CONTROL

There is something in almost all of us that seems to rebel against being controlled by anything or anybody. There are at least two stages of development when this stubborn streak of will seems to be especially visible. The first occurs when children turn two years old. It is no accident that "terrible twos" is a term used by parents to describe strong-willed children. At the age of approximately two years, the child is "terrible" because of an unwillingness to let the parents help them with anything. Independence is all the two year old wants. A child gets frustrated when the parents get in the way. Adolescence is another stage when this need for being in control is especially strong. Think back to when you were an adolescent, or to when you observed other children as teenagers. Are teenagers bull-headed and difficult to control? Do they appear determined to do what they want, regardless of what a more mature and reasonable adult wants them to do? Most people would answer: "Yes, emphatically YES."

Having briefly reviewed behavior during these two periods, are there any other behaviors that appear to you to be equally rebellious? We would like to draw your attention to a comparison between the two mentioned periods and that observed in adult smokers. Your brain has been pampered for years. You responded to its demand anytime it called for nicotine. It seems to enjoy this sense of "being in charge." Suddenly you, as a conscious, mature, intelligent adult, decide to withdraw its supply. How long does it take the brain to toss a temper tantrum? To bring you back to your senses? To prove once again its unwillingness to be controlled by you?

A large percentage of the smokers we have talked to share a common thought about smoking. They feel they must become a nonsmoker because smoking is one of the few things in life they can't seem to control. These people are often quite disciplined. They take pride in being able to do just about anything. They are leaders wherever they go. Other people come to them for advice. They have a sense of mastery over everything except smoking. That bothers them greatly!

Craig was such a person. You would like Craig. He has a pleasing appearance, a quick wit, an obvious high intelligence, and an impish grin that is reserved for special occasions. His description of what happened to him during the Substitution step was very interesting. Craig was having a terrible struggle giving up cigarettes during the evening hours. There was a little voice deep inside that kept whispering advice to him all day. Its advice was:

"I guess you know they are slowly taking everything you like away from you."

"Laws are made to be broken. I don't care how many places post 'No Smoking' signs. Surely you are clever enough to get around some dumb law."

"Have you no memory? You know you gained 30 pounds the last time you tried to quit smoking?"

After considerable debate with this little voice, Craig chose to take control of his smoking. He stopped coming up with excuses about why he was different from everyone else participating in the Cooper/Clayton Method. He quit fighting the logic of providing his brain an alternate form of the nicotine it previously received from cigarettes. He became a nonsmoker on schedule and with relatively little pain.

You have shown, by completing the Replacement, Maintenance I and Elimination I steps, that you are able to take away the control cigarette smoking has exerted over you. That takes a lot of courage and discipline. You shown you can do it. Nobody else did it for you. You deserve a rest from the struggle of eliminating smoking, a reward for success, and a time to prepare for the last step in your journey — breaking the dependence on nicotine.

MAINTENANCE II - The Second Component of Step 3.

The next stage is called Maintenance II. It is the part of your journey designed to provide a chance for you to regroup. This time allows you to stretch your legs and clear your head for the next phase of the trip. The Maintenance II step lasts 2-4 weeks.

This part of the Cooper/Clayton Method is specifically designed to allow three final adjustments to occur: (1) to get your brain totally comfortable receiving nicotine as a temporary aid from Nicoderm® (nicotine transdermal system) as opposed to smoking; (2) to train it to totally accept nicotine in a steady flow, as opposed to the quick jolts you received when cigarette smoke was inhaled; and (3) to continue to modify the remaining physical, psychological, and social aspects of smoking.

STILL DEPENDENT ON NICOTINE

This step in the process of becoming a nonsmoker should not be started without some planning. You must constantly remember that although you are not smoking, you have not stopped taking nicotine. You are receiving approximately 14 mg of nicotine a day from Nicoderm. The primary difference between now and 6-8 weeks ago is the way your body gets its hourly allowance of nicotine. It is absorbing nicotine through the skin, rather than from the lungs.

Relatively speaking, most participants in the Cooper/Clayton Method agree that the intense desire for nicotine slowly subsides during the Maintenance I and Maintenance II stages. This allows you to increase your resolve to be a nonsmoker. This resolve becomes stronger each and every day.

A common occurrence at about this stage is for the ex-smoker to get in a rush to drop the nicotine patch. If you have questions, such as the ones we describe below, check with your prescribing physician or dentist. We suspect their response will be similar to ours.

Question:

"What happens when I continue to use Nicoderm?

"Will I become dependent on Nicoderm?"

Your physician or dentist will determine how long you use the nicotine replacement therapy. Remember, you became dependent on nicotine from your cigarettes. Your doctor or dentist will assist you to wean yourself from Nicoderm. Nevertheless, let us address your questions, since you will probably have some concerns.

81

You have read far enough by now to know that we will not "put you down." However, the only possible answer to a question about whether using Nicoderm® (nicotine transdermal system) for 10-16 weeks will harm you, is to ask another question: "Compared to what?"

Will 10-16 weeks of Nicoderm harm you compared to 30 cigarettes of high nicotine and tar content each day for the remaining years of your life?

Will 10-16 weeks of Nicoderm harm you compared to the hundreds of gasses you inhale from a cigarette that burns at 1600 to 1800 degrees Fahrenheit when you draw on it?

We would guess that responses to these questions are persuasive in one direction. Feel free to discuss these questions with the physician or dentist who is providing your prescription for the nicotine replacement therapy. We suggest that you consider some of the key features of the Cooper/Clayton Method in reaching an answer as to whether continued use of Nicoderm will be harmful to you. The goal of this comprehensive behavioral smoking-cessation program is to assist you to be a nonuser of nicotine, and to minimize the probability of relapse at some future date.

If your smoking and Nicoderm use pattern was similar to Joan's, here is what you might expect. If Joan used one 21 mg Nicoderm patch every day for 6 weeks, that is 21 mg a day times 42 days (6 weeks) equals 882 mg of nicotine. If she also used 2 weeks of the 14 mg Nicoderm patch (196 mg of nicotine) and 2 weeks of the 7 mg Nicoderm patch (98 mg of nicotine), that would be a total of 1,176 mg of nicotine from Nicoderm. That is considerably less nicotine than Joan would have consumed had she continued smoking 30 cigarettes per day. For example, several popular cigarettes in the United States are rated at 0.7 milligrams of nicotine. David Sachs M.D., a noted researcher, states that smokers learn to extract approximately 1 milligram of nicotine from cigarettes of this or an even lower rating. They do this by inhaling more deeply and holding the smoke in their lungs longer than the test machine does. Thus, Joan and any other person smoking 30 cigarettes a day, extracting 1 milligram of nicotine from each cigarette, will absorb a total of 2,100 milligrams of nicotine over 10 weeks. This is almost 80% more than the 1,176 milligrams Joan absorbed from Nicoderm. In addition, Joan would have pulled a lot of noxious gasses, such as carbon monoxide into her lungs in order to get the nicotine had she continued using cigarettes as her nicotine source.

The comparison of potential damage or costs that may occur from using Nicoderm for 10 to 16 weeks, to what may occur from using cigarettes over the same length of time, appears to us to be lopsided. However, you are the only person who can make a decision about this issue. In addition, the probability that you will totally remove nicotine from your life is increased when your follow this program to first eliminate cigarettes and then eliminate nicotine.

Remember, with the Cooper/Clayton Method, the fourth step involves backing off Nicoderm, and thus breaking your dependence on nicotine.

IF YOU ARE STILL CONCERNED ABOUT THE POTENTIAL HARMFUL EFFECT OF USING NICODERM OVER A PERIOD OF 10 to 16 WEEKS, there are health professionals in your community who can provide answers. We encourage you to consult your physician, dentist, or pharmacist for additional information about Nicoderm. For your benefit, the Appendix of this book contains the Product Information that Marion Merrell Dow Inc. places in each box of Nicoderm.

Key Points to Remember:

1. Your brain is still dependent on nicotine during the Maintenance II step.

2. It is receiving its supply in a different manner.

3. You have given up smoking cigarettes.

As you continue to evaluate the long-term effects of cigarette smoking compared to the use of Nicoderm, keep these three points in mind.

IMPORTANCE OF THE LEVEL OF NICOTINE
IN THE BLOOD

When Joan was smoking, there was a sharp peak in the level of nicotine in her blood seven seconds after she took a puff and inhaled the smoke. With Nicoderm® (nicotine transdermal system), it is not possible for Joan to obtain the peaks in the level of blood nicotine that occurred when she smoked. She found that she was comfortable getting a steady release of nicotine into the blood throughout the day. This surprised her to some extent.

She also discovered two other important lessons about getting nicotine from a skin patch. First, one day Joan was in a big hurry and forgot to take the old patch off when she applied the new patch. About noon of that day she began to get nauseated. She was getting nicotine from the new patch she had applied right before getting into the shower as well as from the old patch from the previous day. Once she took the old patch off, things settled down. Second, on another hurried day, Joan took the old patch off and forgot to put a new one on. By mid-morning she was experiencing nicotine withdrawal symptoms and realized the importance of following a schedule for using Nicoderm. She made a mental note to put a nicotine patch on her bedside table tonight to remind her tomorrow morning. She now knew that her body was still dependent on nicotine, at least for a little while longer.

MAINTENANCE II: BASKING IN THE GLORY OF VICTORY—REMINDERS THAT THE STRUGGLE IS NOT OVER

This is the point of highest joy. You have made it through another milestone of the Cooper/Clayton Method. This is when you feel a sense of exhilaration, of accomplishment. Your self-esteem is high. You feel that you can conquer almost anything.

However, don't be surprised if you also experience some things that are a temporary nuisance. During Maintenance II, some of the less-than-positive things you will experience are continued thoughts about cigarettes, losing your cheering section, and a feeling your body is still in second gear, refusing to go into high gear.

1. THINKING ABOUT CIGARETTES.

It is one thing to no longer be smoking, it is quite another to purge the mind of all of the pleasant memories of smoking. Several times during the two weeks of Maintenance II, you will find yourself thinking how nice it would be to have a cigarette. That will usually occur at times when you would normally have smoked. Don't be surprised if you dream about smoking, even vivid dreams. This is a natural part of the process of becoming a nonsmoker. Remember, you are not actually craving the nicotine in the cigarettes, that is being taken care of temporarily by Nicoderm. Your need at this point is more mental or emotional than physical. That is why being a part of a comprehensive behavioral smoking-cessation program like the Cooper/Clayton Method is so important. It allows you to make the emotional adjustments slowly, and with support, as you slowly wean your body off nicotine.

2. LOSING YOUR CHEERING SECTION.

Your thoughts of smoking will begin to subside, but so does the support of those who have been encouraging you. Nonsmokers don't really understand smokers, no matter how sincerely and hard they try. This is a common complaint of persons going through any smoking-cessation program. Nonsmokers may be and usually are "very supportive" while you are in the Qualification and the Substitution/Maintenance I phases. Now that you have been off cigarettes for over six weeks, they assume you have made it "all the way." They don't understand the hold nicotine addiction can have over a person. All they know is that six or so weeks ago you were a smoker — now you aren't. Therefore, don't expect a great deal of continuing support from your nonsmoking friends. YOU know that you are still in the process of becoming a nonsmoker, and that is enough at this point. The next statement we must make saddens us. We have observed that some of your "smoking buddies" might like to see you fail. That may be conscious or unconscious on their part. We suspect they "die" a little bit each time a "smoking buddy" is able to lay cigarettes down while they continue to smoke.

3. TEMPORARY LOW ENERGY LEVEL.

One of the actions nicotine has on the body is to stimulate the central nervous system. This makes you feel more alert. Your idling speed is higher. Your body's basic metabolic rate is higher.

Although you are still getting nicotine from Nicoderm® (nicotine transdermal system), you have reduced your daily consumption of nicotine. You have lost the benefit of this artificial boost. You feel draggy. You feel you are in second gear and can't shift into high gear. Don't despair! This feeling lasts only a short period of time. Normally, in four to six weeks it should disappear entirely. If it does not, check with your physician to see if some medication you are taking needs to be adjusted since you no longer are smoking. However, you should know that most individuals start feeling more energetic than usual.

Assuming there is no cause other than the absence of high nicotine levels, there are several ways you can accelerate your return to a normal energy level. The simplest change you can make is to look for activities that cause a natural rise in your body's metabolic rate. Walk a couple of miles every day. Stop dodging stairs, you can usually beat the elevator anyway. Stop parking on the curb at the grocery. Park 20 rows away. The walk will no longer leave you winded. All those years you shunned physical activity are now history. Your breathing is probably improved. In fact, preliminary data from a study being conducted at the University of Kentucky show marked improvements in pulmonary functioning after smoking-cessation among smokers who were selected because of impaired pulmonary function. Look for natural ways to "rev up" your body's metabolism. You no longer have to use a drug such as nicotine to feel alert.

QUESTION:

When will I quit thinking about smoking and cigarettes?

Margie said it best: "Your craving turns into yearning." Craving implies a strong, almost overpowering sensation that cries out for help. Yearning is a wistful sort of feeling that speaks to you, but softly. You still think about smoking. You still think at certain times about how good a cigarette would taste, but you resist. You have made it this far. You are

86

too smart to throw all of the effort you expended during the Substitution and Maintenance I steps down the tube. During Maintenance II, you are more than six weeks away from smoking cigarettes. Thoughts about smoking are occurring less frequently and, when they occur, they are less intense.

The second stage of not thinking about cigarettes occurs more slowly. However, the people who have followed the Cooper/Clayton Method report that this desire does wane, and for many smokers, is almost totally eliminated after 1 to 2 years. Tom said that about the only time he thinks about smoking is when he runs into one of the people using the Cooper/Clayton Method. However, for the 12 months after he became a non-smoker, he thought about smoking. The intensity of these fleeting thoughts was reduced the further he got from the day he made the switch in how he gave his brain nicotine. Most participants report that in one year, after going completely around the calendar one time as a nonsmoker, they seldom think about cigarettes. This is reported by the large majority of those who have used the Cooper/Clayton Method. It must be a phenomenon resembling the adjustment an individual makes after suffering the loss of a loved one. You must go through every "special occasion," such as Christmas, Thanksgiving, birthdays, anniversaries, etc., without your special friend — the cigarettes — then memories diminish rapidly. We suspect that the speed with which these thoughts about smoking go away is directly related to how dependent you were on nicotine, and how many aspects of your life revolved around smoking. The important point to remember is that you have won the most important battle. Stopping the smoking BEHAVIOR is much more difficult than stopping the THOUGHTS about smoking. If the behavior can be extinguished, you can be assured that it is possible to extinguish thoughts about smoking.

MAINTAINING SUCCESS DURING MAINTENANCE

Success and the recognition that goes with it is something all of us desire. More often than not, success is nothing more than adhering to a plan that is well-designed. This plan should be a road map between where you are and where you want to be. There are several "rules of the road" that must be followed for you to be successful in the Maintenance II step of this program.

RULE 1.

NICODERM® (NICOTINE TRANSDERMAL SYSTEM) IS A PRESCRIPTION DRUG. IT IS MEDICATION. USE IT IN A PATTERNED MANNER LIKE YOU WOULD ANY OTHER MEDICINE. AS WITH ALL PRESCRIPTION DRUGS, FOLLOW THE INSTRUCTIONS FROM YOUR PHYSICIAN OR DENTIST.

If you think of your dependence on nicotine as an addiction, Nicoderm is the medication that has been prescribed by your doctor as an aid to smoking-cessation for the relief of withdrawal symptoms. The Cooper/Clayton Method provides the instructions you are to follow to get well. This is particularly important during the Maintenance II phase. There is a tendency with users of Nicoderm, just as there is with users of other prescription drugs, for a little self-diagnosis and self-medication. Have you ever been told by a physician or dentist to: "Take this until all of it is gone." Then, after you begin to feel better, you return to your normal round of activities. You say to yourself: "I feel so good I'm not going to keep taking this medicine. I don't need it." This is a normal reaction. We all seem to have a built-in resistance to taking medication, once we are feeling better. THOSE WHO ARE THE MOST SUCCESSFUL USE NICODERM LONG ENOUGH TO DISTANCE THEMSELVES FROM CIGARETTES AS THEY BREAK THEIR DEPENDENCE ON NICOTINE GRADUALLY.

RULE 2.

USING NICODERM ON A SCHEDULE IS AN IMPORTANT PREDICTOR OF SUCCESS DURING MAINTENANCE II.

The key to success during Maintenance II is to take Nicoderm as if you were treating a roaring infection — a condition that requires adequate blood levels of an antibiotic. You don't run the risk of a flare up or a relapse. Heavy smokers, and those who have heavy nicotine dependence, used significantly more nicotine during any single day than the situational smoker. Remember, you spent many years teaching yourself how to use nicotine. A few weeks will be necessary to re-teach your brain to accept smaller and smaller amounts of nicotine until, finally, your brain accepts zero nicotine as normal.

RULE 3.

DON'T GET IN A HURRY.

The Cooper/Clayton Method first gets you to change your source of nicotine. Next, you are weaned away from nicotine. During the Maintenance II phase you are probably using a 14 mg Nicoderm patch. Fourteen mg of nicotine is generally less than one-half the amount of nicotine you were getting from cigarettes, if you were a 30 a day smoker. For the situational smoker or the regimented smoker, the same word of caution is appropriate. Check your smoking pattern determined during weeks one and two. You were using cigarettes as a reward. With the Nicoderm patch, there is no "reward" in using nicotine — it just seeps into your bloodstream throughout the day.

THE END OF MAINTENANCE II:
PREPARING FOR THE FINAL PART OF THE JOURNEY

The two to four weeks of Maintenance II will go by quickly. You will discover with each day that you are getting stronger in your resolve to be a nonsmoker. Every day is a victory that puts you further and further away from cigarettes. In fact, at the end of Maintenance II, it will be eight to twelve weeks since your last cigarette. The thoughts about cigarettes will more and more often be felt as just a passing thought or a yearning ("Wouldn't it be nice to have a cigarette now?"). As soon as the thought passes, you will be thinking: "I don't smoke anymore, isn't that great?"

Another thing you will notice happening during the final days of Maintenance II concerns the social aspects of smoking. You will seldom reach for your pocket or purse. You and your body are getting used to not having the cigarette as a crutch. You are discovering that your hands are not awkward. They do seem to belong to you.

Finally, during this last part of the Maintenance period, the victory you have won over cigarettes becomes something you will begin to cherish, internally, intrinsically, privately. The applause from your family, friends, and co-workers will have died down. The praise you receive will come from within. At least once a day stop and reflect on your journey. ENJOY a moment of quiet SELF-PRAISE. You did it, you deserve it.

RECOMMENDATIONS:

At the end of the Maintenance II phase you will be 8-12 weeks away from cigarettes. By now, some of the beneficial effects of not smoking will become apparent. You will probably notice that foods are beginning to taste better. You recognize the herbs and spices. Your taste buds are recovering. You will begin to notice smells that you never before noticed. Many patients report that the sense of smell has improved dramatically. Food smells better. Unfortunately, unpleasant smells are also becoming more intense. The smell of an ashtray filled with cigarette butts becomes offensive to the ex-smoker about this time. One person who completed the Cooper/Clayton Method went to a resort area for the weekend. Shortly after getting into the hotel room she climbed up on the bed to watch the TV. Suddenly, she started sniffing the bedspread and the pillow. The stale tobacco smoke smelled awful to her.

1. Treat yourself to a trip to the dentist. Have your teeth cleaned. Your mouth will feel better and cigarette stains are history for you.

2. Treat yourself to a new start. Take all of the clothes that have been saturated with tobacco smoke to the cleaners. You deserve a clean wardrobe.

3. Get your drapes cleaned and do the same for your carpet, chairs, and sofas.

4. Take your automobile to the car wash. Have it washed and ask them to clean all the brown gunk off the inside of the windows.

5. Ask for "new car" air freshener.

6. Fill your auto ash trays with potpourri. This gives a strong message to those who might be tempted to smoke in your clean smelling automobile.

This is a new beginning for your life. You could be eight to twelve weeks away from being controlled by cigarettes. You are ready to begin the journey to your final destination — that of being a non-user of nicotine. The next part of the journey involves backing off your dependence on nicotine. You have now been victorious over smoking for 8-12 weeks. Percentagewise, the odds that you will be a nonsmoker 1 year from now have improved significantly.

CHAPTER 6
STEP 4. ELIMINATION II AND MAINTENANCE II

In Chapter 3, we said: "A journey is not really a journey, but is a series of short trips." You have now completed three of the four short trips in your journey toward being a nonsmoker. You are not to your final destination, but you can see the finish line from here! Here's a scenario.

You successfully completed the Qualification leg of the journey. It was boring, but necessary to record every cigarette you smoked. You established precisely where you were as a cigarette smoker.

Next, you started and successfully mastered two parts of the journey — Nicotine Replacement and Maintenance I. There were probably times you seriously questioned your sanity. To even consider replacing those essential cigarettes with a nicotine patch probably seemed at times to be one of your dumber ideas. But, you persisted. You gained great confidence during that leg of the journey. You went from "being controlled" to "taking control."

Elimination I and Maintenance II was a relatively easy leg of the journey. The nicotine needs of your brain were being met by Nicoderm® (nicotine transdermal system). Elimination I was probably easier than you expected; going from a 21 mg patch to a 14 mg patch wasn't that big a jump. Your brain accepted a smaller amount of nicotine as "normal." Just 2-4 weeks from now, it will accept zero nicotine as normal! What a great feeling that will be!

The final leg of the journey begins now. Relax. The hard part of the trip is behind you. Follow the instructions in this chapter, and you may become not only a nonsmoker, but a person who no longer needs nicotine to have a good day.

The day you had your last cigarette has probably become a very important anniversary in your life. If asked, you can cite it as readily as you can cite your birthday or social security number. It has become an important milestone in your personal autobiography. It is recorded somewhere in your book.

Now you will reduce your daily intake of nicotine the final time. Just as you made the transition from the cigarette by using the 21 mg nicotine patch for 6-8 weeks, changing to the 14 mg nicotine patch for 2-4 weeks, you are now going to further eliminate nicotine. Starting today, you will start using the 7 mg Nicoderm® (nicotine transdermal system) patch. Your brain has grown accustomed to the relatively level, sustained release of the transdermal patch. It has been 8-12 weeks since your brain had the "hits" of nicotine you formerly gave it when you inhaled cigarette smoke. You have eliminated the strong reinforcing effects of inhaling a drug to provide the brain its daily "needs." Your brain has also accepted the lower amount of nicotine it received from the 14 mg Nicoderm patch. The next 2-4 weeks require minimal adjustment as you reduce the daily dose of nicotine to the 7 mg nicotine patch. At the end of this 2-4 week period you will no longer use Nicoderm.

COMING OFF THE NICOTINE STAIRCASE

When you started smoking you started slowly, a cigarette here, a cigarette there. In those days, you smoked only one or two a day. Then, you began to increase until you got up to about 10 to 12 cigarettes a day. That probably became a plateau until something pushed you into heavier and more frequent use. Eventually, like virtually all smokers, you established a "level of smoking" that became your lifetime pattern. For some, this level is a pack a day —seldom more and almost never any less than that. For others, it is a pack and a half; for still others, two packs. YOU CLIMBED THE CIGARETTE SMOKING/NICOTINE STAIRCASE ONE STEP AT A TIME. However, once you reached a certain level or plateau, you remained there. Your brain began to expect a certain "minimum daily allowance" of nicotine. For how many years have you been giving yourself that dose?

Your brain is still dependent on nicotine. You are still on that nicotine staircase. You were at the top of the stairs for most of the last few years. For Tom it was 36 years. How long were you up there, afraid to try to come down those stairs for fear that you might fail again? During Substitution and Maintenance I you backed down a little, then rested for awhile. During Elimination I and Maintenance II you backed down a little more and then rested again, allowing your brain to accept this new reduced level of nicotine as normal.

THE FINAL LEG ON YOUR JOURNEY — TOTAL VICTORY OVER NICOTINE

Well, the time has come. You walked up, you can walk down. You can continue to reduce your dependence on nicotine. This step lasts 2-4 weeks.

RULE 1.

DON'T RUSH. The "down" staircase is purposefully designed to be gentle.

During this step, you will eliminate nicotine from your life. The same process will be followed whether you are a situational or a regimented smoker. If you are a situational smoker, you will be joining Joan at the appropriate point and eliminating Nicoderm.

To make the Elimination II part of your journey easier to understand, we will visit our friend Joan as she starts down the stairs toward TOTAL removal of nicotine from her life.

STAGES OF ELIMINATION II

It is not possible to predict when changes you will observe during this two to four week period occur. Although the changes among those who stop smoking are very similar, the rate at which they occur is variable.

The response timetable varies considerably even for those who have smoked for similar lengths of time.

The factors which appear to influence how rapidly your body responds to the elimination of nicotine are listed below.

1. The length of time you smoked cigarettes.

2. The number of cigarettes per day you smoked.

3. Your depth of inhalation.

4. The length of time you held the cigarette smoke in your lungs before exhaling.

5. Unknown factors that determined what changes your body made to defend itself from the irritating effects of years of cigarette smoking.

We have helped many smokers become nonsmokers. Most of the behaviors observed are relatively predictable. After observing a few participants, you can anticipate, within reason, what to expect at each of the first 3 steps.

But, our guidelines regarding this final step — Elimination II — will be fairly general. It is NOT that we don't want to be specific. It is only that the experiences of participants in the program are more variable during step 4. Therefore, we have broken the 2-4 weeks of this step into 2 stages.

If you are a heavy smoker, a regimented smoker, you might expect the phases Joan experienced. If you are a situational smoker, smoking perhaps only eight hours or less each day, you can expect to follow only the first phase Joan experienced.

ELIMINATION II STAGE 1.
SENSITIVITY TO CIGARETTE SMOKE
AND A NEW FREEDOM

It wasn't that long ago that smoke-filled rooms would not have bothered you at all. You probably contributed to the smoke. By now, you are becoming acutely aware of cigarette smoke. You find yourself consciously sitting up-stream from smokers. You will probably notice filled ashtrays continue to smell terrible. (They may always have smelled, but your sense of smell probably wasn't as sensitive.) You notice the smell of stale tobacco smoke on the clothes of your smoking friends. You discover how strong a smoker's breath is. Now you realize how nonsmokers must have felt about talking to you when you smoked. Doesn't it feel great to be able to smell again? You didn't realize it, but during all those years of smoking, you were missing out on some wonderful aromas.

One day during a discussion, we described our hypothesis that some heavy smokers may be allergic to cigarette smoke. Or, if not allergic, they may be very sensitive to smoke. Over the years of smoking, they have assaulted that physical sensitivity so much that they are unaware of it. In response to that hypothesis, one participant, Jack, a leading disc jockey in the area, rolled his eyes and said: "You've got to be kidding!" Several weeks later he came into the meeting and said: "You won't believe what happened to me yesterday. I was having dinner with my mother in a restaurant where the air circulation system wasn't working. Suddenly, tears starting rolling from my eyes and wouldn't stop. I looked up and 30 feet away a woman was smoking a cigarette. I was so excited I almost walked across the room to give her a kiss." When you think about it, putting a burning object into your mouth and inhaling the smoke into your lungs is not a "natural" process. It stands to reason that your body will react defensively when something unnatural happens to it. Isn't it great that our bodies so quickly readjust?

During the first part of Elimination II, you may have become very much aware of smoke and your reaction to it. You have joined the "majority."

SIT ANYWHERE YOU WANT.

As a nonsmoker in a world where attitudes about smoking and smokers have been changing dramatically, you know all too well about segregation. Ten or 15 years ago, smokers could go anywhere and sit anywhere in restaurants. Now they have to sit in the "smoking section." If you fly on domestic airplanes regularly you are quite aware that there is no smoking section. Smokers are becoming a segregated minority in public places. Isn't it great that you can now sit anywhere you want in a restaurant?

YOUR VOICE WILL CHANGE.

Have you ever told a small child: "Don't play with fire. Fire is hot. It burns." If you are a parent, these words will sound familiar to you. Fire does burn and cigarettes burn hot. In fact, as we previously stated, the fire at the tip of a burning cigarette is in the range of 1600-1800 degrees Fahrenheit. As you know all too well, the smoke inhaled when you smoke cigarettes is irritating to soft body tissue. Most of us can tell by a hoarse and raspy voice whether a person is a smoker.

The same is true for what is commonly called "smokers cough." When the soft tissues of the tracheobronchial tree are bombarded day-in and day-out for many years with hot cigarette smoke, the bronchial tubes are constantly irritated. Smokers' cough is thus a sign of chronic bronchitis. When you stopped drawing smoke into your lungs every waking hour of every day, the irritation in your bronchial tubes began to clear up. If you have been smoking a long time, don't expect miracles overnight. But, week by week, the cough should get better. So will your voice. It will lose some of its hoarseness and raspiness.

IT'S A JOY, NOT A JOB, TO BREATHE.

Shortness of breath is something that smokers learn to live with. One reason it occurs is oxygen deprivation. The almost hourly inhalation of carbon monoxide by smokers reduces the oxygen carrying capacity of the red blood cells. When you quit smoking, as you did, the red blood cells pick up oxygen instead of carbon monoxide. In fact, for the first time in "forever," you don't shun stairs. When you were a smoker you probably couldn't walk up one flight of stairs without getting winded. Now you can take that flight without a second thought, and the next flight, and the next flight! Isn't that a GREAT feeling?

ELIMINATION II STAGE 2.
IMPROVED APPEARANCE

Perhaps you remember the advertisements for a popular hair preparation, a product for people with gray hair who wanted to return to their original color. The actor in the advertisement applied the product every day, and slowly the color of his hair changed from drab gray to a vibrant and younger looking brown, with just a touch of gray. The boss would appear on the scene, put his hand on the man's shoulder, and say: "Jim, you look great. Have you lost some weight?"

It's normal to want to think we are attractive and look good. As we get older, it is also normal to want to look younger than we are. Men are just as "vain" about appearance as women.

One of the signposts on your journey to being a nonsmoker has to do with appearance. It is not unusual for us to have participants report compliments from family and friends about how good they look, questions about losing weight, or comments such as: "I really like your makeup. Are you using something different?" What has happened is that blood is now flowing, without the vasoconstriction (blood vessel shrinking) to your face and other parts of your body. For the first time in a long time your face doesn't have the look of a smoker.

A NEW IDENTITY AND A NEW ASSURANCE.

During the last step of this method, one of the most favorable signposts is the way you sort people into groups. You have always done this, all of us do. There are males and females; friends, acquaintances, and non-friends; and young people and older people. As you grow older, the boundaries between these categories seem to float somewhat. Remember when you were in your early 20s, and everyone over 30 seemed "old." When you are in your early 30s, people don't seem old until they are about 45. Then when you reach your 40s, older takes on a new meaning. There are also smokers and nonsmokers. Increasingly you think of yourself as a nonsmoker. Doesn't it feel great to think of cigarette smokers as THEM rather than "us?"

A NEW ASSURANCE: I'M PROUD OF ME.

During this portion of your journey, an interesting change occurs. Smokers who never thought they would be able to overcome their addiction to nicotine, "sight victory." The increase in their self-esteem is exciting to behold. You earned it. Enjoy!

HAZARDS ON THE ROAD TO SUCCESS

All of us are familiar with various road signs which alert us to potential dangers that lie ahead.

SLIPPERY WHEN WET

BRIDGES FREEZE BEFORE ROADWAY

FALLING ROCK

DENSE FOG NEXT 5 MILES

They tell us what to expect just ahead, or under varying weather conditions. In reading for a trip, it is not unusual for a traveler to read the weather forecast or tune into the weather channel for an update on conditions at the destination. If someone has recently been on the same journey, we might ask about the trip. However, we are most interested in any appropriate WARNINGS.

In this section we will review two hazards that might arise on your road to success. It is certainly more prudent to anticipate problems and think through what your response will be, rather than being caught "off guard" because of a lack of planning. You wouldn't go on a trip without checking to make sure you have a spare tire and a jack, in case it is needed. The same principle applies with regard to becoming a nonsmoker. There may be hazards that you need to think about ahead of time.

WEIGHT GAIN: A POTENTIAL HAZARD OF QUITTING SMOKING

We live in a very weight conscious society. Some observers claim that there is a "thinness" norm in Western societies that accounts for eating disorders such as anorexia nervosa and bulimia. The first and most often dreaded potential hazard of becoming a nonsmoker is weight gain.

The connection between gaining weight and becoming a nonsmoker is not "in your mind." It is real. Nicotine is an appetite suppressant. It reduces hunger and decreases your "perceived need" for food (Grunberg et al., 1986), it helps reduce the discomfort of being too full and causes the heart to pump faster than it would otherwise (Goodman and Gilman, 1988). Finally, nicotine also causes an increase in the body's resting metabolic rate (Hofstetter, 1986). The fact that the body is not working as hard when you become a nonsmoker means that the body is not burning up calories as fast as it was when you were smoking. Therefore, those calories are more readily converted by the body into fat. Snacking habits you got by with while still smoking may lead to weight gain problems, now that you are a nonsmoker. One of the strongest predictors of weight gain after eliminating cigarettes is weight while still smoking. Sharon Hall, Ph.D., a psychologist at the University of California in San Francisco, and some of her colleagues, have described one reason why there is a connection between weight gain and becoming a nonsmoker.

"Weight problems are usually chronic. They occur in many circumstances in susceptible individuals and are likely to recur. We therefore suggest that weight gain would be more likely in subjects with a history of high body weight and of gaining weight during other quitting attempts."

Drs. Ronald Manley and Frederick Boland, scientists from Canada, described important elements concerning whether some weight gain is too high a price to pay in becoming a nonsmoker. "While weight gain is associated with successful cessation, the amount of weight gain does not support the exaggerated concerns many clients have about weight gain following smoking-cessation."

This is not very reassuring to people who worry about gaining weight when they are no longer smokers. The idea that nicotine might help them keep the pounds off might be a strong inducement to return to smoking. If weight gain is something you worry about as a side effect of becoming a nonsmoker, let us recommend some things which can help you avoid or minimize this problem.

RULE 1.
ADJUST FOR NON-SMOKING STATUS

Studies done on smokers to measure metabolic rate, oxygen consumption, caloric intake and weight showed an interesting pattern. Once off cigarettes, with all other factors held at the same level, the individuals had an excess intake of 200 calories per day. When nothing was done, the individuals started gaining weight. The researchers hypothesized that the weight gain would continue until the effort of carrying around the excess weight (22 pounds) used up the 200 excess calories. The weight gain is not necessary, however. An ex-smoker has a choice of two ways to prevent weight gain. The extra 200 calories could be compensated for by burning off calories through exercise, such as walking two miles. It could also be compensated for by deleting 200 calories of intake per day, such as dropping two cans of soft drink or two slices of buttered bread.

Contrary to popular misconceptions, it is not necessary to gain weight after giving up cigarettes. Most individuals following the Cooper/Clayton Method report that, by following a reasonable eating schedule and the guidelines in this book, permanent weight gain is not a problem. Occasionally, five to 10 pounds is added during the 24 week program. Once people are off nicotine totally, they begin to address the modest weight gain. Many report a loss of three to five pounds by the end of the first year off cigarettes, and report an overall net gain of only four to six pounds after becoming a nonsmoker.

RULE 2.
SYSTEMATICALLY REDUCE FOOD INTAKE.

We will assume that your balance of protein, fat, and carbohydrates is adequate and your weight is stabilized before you start the Cooper/Clayton Method. This book is not written to address the issue of nutritional balance, important as that is. If you have any questions about the adequacy of your diet, we strongly urge you to consult with someone knowledgeable in that area. Also, many good books exist on this subject. This will allow us to concentrate on the volume of food you consume, with only a few suggestions about the types of food you eat.

A major key to controlling weight when you become a nonsmoker is to cut back on food intake. As you are going through this last step, serve yourself at every meal just as you always have done. Then, purposefully leave a small portion of each vegetable, meat, or whatever, on the plate. Many of us eat excessively because we have fallen victim to the "clean plate" syndrome. The seeds for this syndrome were sowed by our parents who used to tell us: "Good children clean their plates." As a trusting child, you ATE! You stuffed yourself! You developed a behavior pattern that may still be with you as an adult.

What is that pattern? "Anything that gets on my plate is fair game!" As children we learned to put enough food on our plates to provide adequate "fuel" for vigorous activities such as kickball, tag, hide-and-seek, and pick-up basketball. For many years, we ate to fuel our body's growth. It takes lots of raw materials to make a little person become a tall

102

person. Unfortunately, when we consume the same amount of "fuel" as adults, we create a problem. We have stopped playing kickball and have become considerably less active. The fuel that once helped us grow vertically, now makes us grow sideways. We become all hips and tummy. When we stop using nicotine, our appetite improves. We then pour in a little more "fuel." Our body, in reality, needs "less" fuel. Thus, weight gain begins to change from a nuisance to a hazard.

The way to deal with this hazard can be very simple. Regardless of what your parents told you, DON'T CLEAN YOUR PLATE. That was good advice they gave you when you were age four, it met your body's needs. At age 40, it is terrible advice. At 50, it is downright risky. There is an alternative. Put the normal amount of food on your plate during the six to eight weeks of Substitution and Maintenance I. During the first week, leave one teaspoonful of food on your plate each meal.

During the next week, leave a second teaspoonful of food. During the following week, leave a 3rd teaspoonful of food. Finally, during the fourth week of Maintenance II, leave a 4th teaspoonful of food on the plate when you are finished. By this time, you will be able to serve yourself four teaspoons less food each meal and still eat adequately. Your new eating behavior will become a useful adjunct to your nonsmoking life-style. Now, we know you think we are encouraging waste — that parental admonition is still there, isn't it? Remember, after "Clean your plate," we received another piece of wisdom from our parents —"Waste not, want not!" We don't want to start a family feud, but we feel your mother will understand if you lighten up a little bit on advice she gave you at 2, 3, and 4, if at 20, 30, and 40, it is no longer appropriate.

This runs counter to all our early training. We must realize that, in the long run, it is NOT wasteful. When you complete the Cooper/Clayton Method in Week 24, you will have reduced your normal food intake by four teaspoons each meal. This reduction represents about a 20 percent reduction in the amount of food you formerly ate. Not only will you help control your weight, you will probably save tons of food over your entire lifetime.

So, from this point on, serve yourself the reduced amount of food. This should more than justify your "temporary" wastefulness while adjusting your food intake. By the end of the entire 24 weeks, you should know exactly how much food to put on your plate.

RULE 3.
STOP EATING BEFORE THAT FULL FEELING, NOT AFTER

If you train your stomach to accept smaller amounts of food, it will soon accept the smaller amounts as normal. If you eat until you are full, your stomach will stretch to accommodate your eating habits. Once stretched, it will require larger amounts of food to accomplish the full feeling. You want to get your stomach to accept a more modest definition of "full."

You have conquered cigarette smoking and are in the process of giving up your dependence on nicotine. If you can be victorious over these things, you can be successful in not gaining weight.

Jacquelyn Rogers, Ph.D., had the following to say in an article on tobacco in a 1981 book entitled "Behavior in Excess."

"Some smokers gain weight as an excuse to resume smoking: 'I'd rather die of lung cancer than have a heart attack from obesity.' However, many smokers deal with weight gain in a positive manner: 'If I can quit smoking, I can do anything. When I've got smoking licked, I'll deal with the weight gain.' This is an ideal attitude."

(Again, the word quitting is a direct quote, not our choice of words).

We agree wholeheartedly with Dr. Rogers. You overcame smoking, you can conquer the problem of gaining weight that sometimes occurs after giving up nicotine.

RULE 4.
TAKE TWICE AS LONG TO EAT

Eating rapidly is a habit. You probably developed such a habit as a child. Many times hours are spent preparing a feast, and ten minutes are spent consuming it. What a waste! When you stop smoking, your appetite may increase. Also, your senses of smell and taste will improve. Enjoy! Slow down! If you will take twice as long to eat a meal, chew twice as many times, you will win two ways. First, you will satisfy your sense of improved appetite by tasting the food for an extended time. Second, you will mix saliva more thoroughly with the food and improve digestion, especially of starches. While eating more slowly, you should also increase your consumption of non-caloric liquids. Beverages such as water or artificially sweetened drinks will contribute to your sense of fullness and minimally affect your calorie total for the day.

Tom found it especially helpful to sip carbonated water, such as club soda, with his food. The carbon dioxide bubbles resulted in a sense of fullness, but contributed absolutely nothing in the way of calories.

RULE 5.
EATING LESS HELPS YOU FORGET AFTER MEAL CIGARETTES

As mentioned, nicotine increases the rhythmic contractions of the small intestine. Smokers have learned that by quickly smoking a couple of cigarettes after over eating, they can speed up intestinal contraction. Now that you are not smoking, the overfull feeling keeps reminding you that something is missing. Stopping short of the full feeling makes dropping the after dinner cigarette easier to cope with.

RULE 6.
SEEK NUTRITIONAL COUNSELING IF NECESSARY.

Some people are more comfortable with a more structured weight control program. If this is your choice, many fine centers exist to help you. Craig, who overcame that "little voice," joined such a weight control program to coincide with his progress through the Cooper/Clayton Method. When he had previously tried to become a nonsmoker, it was not unusual for him to quickly gain 30 to 40 pounds. This time, he gave up smoking and lost 16 pounds during the 24 week program.

This book will not devote a lot of space to nutritional guides. One food product should be discussed to help the new nonsmoker minimize weight gain. The American diet is generally excessively high in fat content. One gram of fat contains nine calories, while one gram of protein or carbohydrate contains only four calories. In addition, nutritionists have discovered that it only requires five percent of the calories in fat to metabolize this food. It requires 15% of the calories in either protein or carbohydrate to metabolize these foods.

Also, limiting dietary fat calories to 20% of total food calories is a good target. A book titled "One Meal At A Time" (W.W. Norton and Company, New York) by Martin Katahn, Ph.D., is an excellent source of information about ways to choose foods that are less likely to result in weight problems for the individual who wants to limit body weight.

RULE 7.
FIND A PROFITABLE USE FOR THE TIME
YOU ONCE SPENT SMOKING

If you formerly smoked 30 cigarettes a day, with an average burn time of five minutes per cigarette, you invested 150 minutes each day in smoking. WOW!, that's a lot of time. Let's see if we can find a profitable use for that time before it is lost.

It is generally accepted that a two-mile brisk walk each day is very helpful in maintaining good muscle tone. It is also beneficial to the cardiovascular system. Another advantage is the calories that will be burned off during this walk. We can think of no better way to "reinvest" 45 to 60 of those minutes than treating yourself to a brisk, two-mile walk each day. An added benefit of this walk will be improved efficiency of your breathing mechanism, enabling you to take full advantage of the oxygen you breath in. After the many years you smoked, suffering chronic oxygen deprivation, this may be a very pleasant change in the quality of your life. You deserve this positive change.

RULE 8.
LEARN TO HANDLE STRESS WITHOUT NICOTINE

The modern world seems to be filled with stressful situations that result in high levels of stress. There is seemingly so much emphasis put on success and on meeting unreasonable deadlines. We always seem to be in a hurry and overscheduled. It is life in the fast lane. Many of us seem to go from one crisis to another, and, we usually thrive on it.

Sometimes, however, the pressures seem to exceed our capacity to adjust. It is then that we become "up tight."

How many times have you heard someone say: "I smoke to cope with the stress in my life. Whenever I have a crisis, those cigarettes are my best friend." Perhaps you have said something similar. By now, you have learned that cigarettes were not responsible for your ability to solve problems — you solved your problems with your experience, your intelligence, and your ability to cope with change. The only way cigarettes assisted was by helping you relax. There are many other less harmful ways to relax.

You have completed 12 weeks (e.g., 2 weeks recording plus 10 to 12 weeks on Nicoderm® (nicotine transdermal system) using a Method that has helped break your dependence on nicotine. You have broken the mechanical habit of reaching for that pack of cigarettes every 30 minutes or so. The things that used to be automatically associated with smoking, such as driving or finishing a good meal, are no longer with you. They belong to the past.

However, just because you were able to conquer your nicotine dependence, doesn't mean that you will be free from the crises of life. They remain. What has changed is the way you will cope with problems. You have learned during this 12 to 14 week period that problems can be dealt with effectively if they are broken down into smaller problems. You have learned that YOUR ABILITIES and not the CIGARETTES are the solution to your problems. Cigarettes were part of the problem, not the solution. You were controlled by nicotine and smoking. Now, you are in control of your life.

When you are faced with a crisis or feel that the pressure is becoming unbearable; remind yourself of your victories over smoking. Think back to how stressed you felt during the Substitution and Maintenance I steps of this program. You resisted returning to cigarettes then. Resist the temptation now.

A CAVEAT

The 10 to 16 weeks since you smoked seems like a long time. It only seems that way because you were so conscious of smoking and your efforts during every waking hour (and even during a few of your dreaming moments). In reality, you have been a nonsmoker a relatively brief period. If you had smoked 20 years for example, the 10 to 16 weeks as a nonsmoker must be compared to your over 1,000 weeks as a smoker. There is a risk now to think, "Now I have won the battle, I am now able to have just one cigarette." Our strong advice to you is DON'T! Don't risk stirring up all those memories. Enjoy your current life as a nonsmoker and it will continue to pay you dividends.

THE END OF THIS JOURNEY IS THE BEGINNING OF THE REST OF YOUR LIFE AS A NONSMOKER

Everything worth doing or worth having takes time, energy, and sacrifice. The signposts we described are just a few of the positive benefits you have received and will be receiving as you continue your journey toward being a nonsmoker. The further you move away from cigarette smoking, the stronger should be your resolve never to smoke again. As you go through the two to four weeks of the final step, giving up nicotine, the craving for nicotine should become just a very faint yearning. This yearning will appear only occasionally, and it will become less and less intense with each passing day and week. You will totally eliminate nicotine at the end of this last two to four weeks of using the 7 mg Nicoderm® (nicotine transdermal system) patch.

Your sense of accomplishment and pride in self will be increasing, not in great leaps, but in quiet steps of confidence. The reality of what you have done in taking control over this addiction will sink in. The final victory over nicotine — achieved when you have gone through the entire 24 weeks — yields a satisfaction that is difficult to describe. It will mean something different for each and every person who has made that journey successfully.

In the final chapter we want to review that journey with you. We want you to put your victories into perspective and ask yourself WHAT you have learned and HOW it can be applied to other areas of your life. The principles that serve as the foundation for the Cooper/Clayton Method are

108

not limited just to winning your battle with cigarettes. They are general enough to apply to solving any problem with which you are faced. In Chapter 8, we will examine these principles in more detail.

CHAPTER 7

Step 5. RELAPSE PREVENTION

You have completed the first phase of the Cooper/Clayton Method to become a nonsmoker. That 12 to 14 week period looked like a terribly long time when you started, didn't it? As you reflect back, we bet you didn't think you would succeed. You did, and you should be very proud of yourself. Now that you have become a nonsmoker, you are beginning Step 5 of the Cooper/Clayton Method. This step is officially 6 to 12 weeks long. In reality, it is much longer. It lasts the rest of your life. Only the formal part is 6 to 12 weeks.

Writer Mark Twain is credited with saying, "Giving up smoking is one of the easiest things I did. I've done it a thousand times." Any smoker who has attempted numerous times to become a nonsmoker can probably identify with Mr. Twain.

The relapse rates for those who have attempted to eliminate alcohol, heroin and nicotine from their lives is almost identical (Surgeon General, The Health Consequences of Smoking: Nicotine Addiction, 1988, Chapter 7). Many succeed in becoming nonusers over the short term. Long term abstinence, however, is a totally different thing.

Figure 7.1 shows abstinence rates at various times. For those who were successful abstainers at week three, a high percentage of them had resumed use of their drug (drugs) of choice by week six.

In order to increase your chances to remain a nonsmoker, it will help to review human behavior in general. It will also help to look at cigarette smoking as one element of human behavior.

Let's begin by stating a couple of general rules about why we act like we do:

Relapse Rates - Addicting Drugs

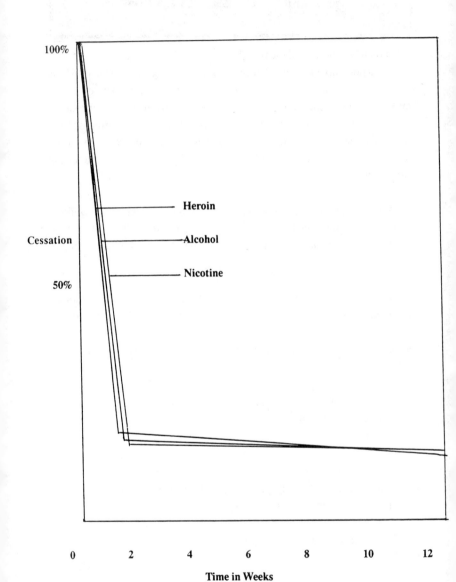

Figure 7-1

GENERAL RULES: NEED DRIVEN BEHAVIOR

**1. Our behavior consists of the sum total
of acts we find rewarding.
2. People do not continue to practice non-rewarding behavior long term.**

Why then does a 13-year-old nonsmoker, become a 14-year-old smoker? It is probably because something happened to cause smoking to become more rewarding than nonsmoking for the individual.

If this is true, then the next question would have to be, what motivation drives our behavior?

The research by Maslow, Hersberg, Lichtenstein and others indicates we behave in a given manner to meet certain needs. Some of the more compelling needs can be seen in Figure 7.2. This circle, showing pie shape wedges, represents the needs in general that drive our behavior. In other words, we act as we do to meet our needs for survival, to be loved, to feel important, to achieve and to meet our spiritual needs. Figure 7.3 shows how the pie wedges might look at age 14. The need to be loved and to feel important dominate. The peer pressure is almost overwhelming. At the same time, the survival and spiritual needs often take secondary importance. Thus, because of a need to impress peers and to feel more mature, the 14-year-old assumes the behavior of smoker to more nearly meet the needs of a 14-year-old.

At age 41, or 51, or 61, this behavior must be re-examined. It must be re-examined, however, based on the needs of the mature adult. Figure 7.4 shows how the needs of this age, with the resulting maturity, have changed. The need for survival and spiritual needs have expanded, while typically the need to be loved and need to feel important have been reduced in size.

Examining Figure 7.4 to determine the needs that drive the behavior of the mature adult, would probably lead the individual to reassess smoking as a desirable or rewarding behavior.

A strong case can be made for the fact that, for the 41-year-old (or 35-year-old, 45-year-old, etc.), becoming a nonsmoker is a more reasonable

Need Driven Behavior

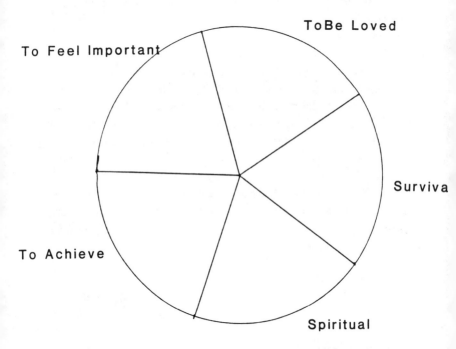

Figure 7-2

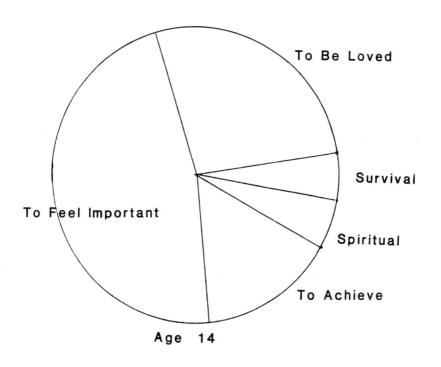

To Be Loved

Survival

Spiritual

To Achieve

To Feel Important

Age 14

Figure 7-3

115

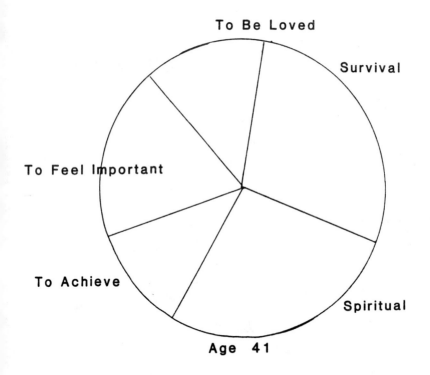

To Be Loved

Survival

To Feel Important

To Achieve

Spiritual

Age 41

Figure 7-4

116

Cooper/Clayton Method
to Stop Smoking
826 Glendover
Lexington, Kentucky 40502

Order Form

Please send me the following Cooper/Clayton Materials:

_____ Single copies of the Cooper/Clayton Book   ($12 per book) _____

_____ Packets (6 copies) of the Cooper/Clayton Book @ $66 ($11 per book) _____

_____ Dozen Copies of the Cooper/Clayton Book @ $120   ($10 per book) _____

_____ Copies of the Cooper/Clayton Video Tape   @ $175 ea. _____
   (Training Sites Only)

_____ Copies of the Cooper/Clayton Leader Resource Book   @ $75 ea. _____
   (Training Sites Only)

SubTotal _____

Shipping Charges — $ 12 to $ 99 - Add $4   Shipping _____

$100 to $199 - Add $6

$200 up - Add $8   **Total** _____

(Kentucky Residents Add 6% Sales Tax)

Ship the materials to me as follows:

Your Name   _____

Your Address   _____

Your City, State, Zip _____

Your Signature _____

behavior than continuing to smoke. This is due to the fact that nonsmoking should more nearly meet the individual's needs for survival, to be loved, to feel important, to achieve and to meet spiritual needs than does continuing to smoke. When the individual reaches this conclusion, the short term behavior of relapsing to smoking a cigarette, which will be extinguished in five minutes, is looked at totally differently.

The new nonsmoker can compare the short term "pleasure" of one cigarette and the satisfaction of a lifetime as a nonsmoker.

During the next 6-12 weeks, the following events typically occur:

1. The smell of cigarette smoke on the breath or in the clothes or hair of a smoker may become progressively more distasteful.

2. You may find you slowly lose your desire for cigarettes, and become very sensitive to the smell of "old" cigarette smoke.

3. Your thoughts of cigarettes occur less frequently. Also, the thought duration, when it occurs, is much briefer.

4. Your identity of yourself as a nonsmoker becomes stronger. You think more of yourself as a nonsmoker, and less as an ex-smoker.

The long term benefits of remaining a nonsmoker become quite clear and make you ask the question —

"Is one cigarette worth risking all I have gained?"

The answer will be, in all probability, a resounding — "No!"

5. You may say to yourself: "I have gained back my self respect, and taken control of a drug that formerly controlled me, and I like it this way. I can more nearly meet my adult needs by remaining a nonsmoker."

When this new manner of looking at smoking becomes the dominant behavior, the individual is better prepared to continue to make the more healthy decision of continued abstinence from cigarettes.

6. The cues and triggers that remind you of cigarettes have diminished considerably. You can now go for whole days without strong memories of cigarettes surfacing.

7. Your enhanced sense of self-worth grows even stronger. You have taken control of an aspect of your life that formerly dominated you. You may still be addicted to nicotine, but you have retrained your brain to accept zero nicotine each day as normal. You have proven what behavioral scientists have known for years — an ignored behavior is discarded. Smoking behavior has been discarded and the newer, more healthy behavior of nonsmoker introduced.

Congratulations!

CHAPTER 8

THE COOPER/CLAYTON METHOD
TO BECOME A NONSMOKER

WHERE DO WE GO FROM HERE?

INTRODUCTION

YOU are to be commended!

YOU have overcome a problem that compromises the health of more than 50 million U.S. citizens alone. The group, of which you were "formerly" a member, smokes 600 billion cigarettes every year. The figure had been decreasing, but it has recently stabilized.

We promised you in Chapter 1 that this book would address the positive aspects of giving up smoking cigarettes. We made no attempt to point out the negative health effects of smoking. However, now that you have succeeded in first changing your source of nicotine from cigarettes to Nicoderm® (transdermal nicotine system) and, by now, have eliminated nicotine totally from your life, it is appropriate that we celebrate your renewed health.

One positive way to celebrate is to reflect on the physical improvements you experienced following your having stopped smoking cigarettes. Dr. Tom Ferguson has written an excellent book, "The Smoker's Book of Health" (G.P. Putnam's Sons, 1987), that describes in detail some of the positive changes you have already or will experience during the first year after you give up cigarettes. They are:

1. The carbon monoxide level in your blood returns to normal in less than 24 hours after you smoke your last cigarette.

2. The heart rate slows.

119

3. Your peripheral circulation improves.

4. Your breathing becomes easier in 2 to 3 weeks.

5. Your body's immune system improves in 3 months.

6. The heart returns to nearly normal within 12 months.

7. You reduce your risk of heart disease by 90% within the first year after you give up cigarettes.

8. Your stamina improves in the first 2 to 3 months after giving up smoking.

Giving up cigarettes is one thing. Remaining a nonsmoker for the rest of your life requires some special effort on your part. Although the relapse rate is very low among participants in the Cooper/Clayton Method, we urge you to do whatever is necessary to retain your current status. As nonsmokers, participants have found it very helpful to read Dr. Ferguson's book, "The Smoker's Book of Health." His description of some of the health consequences of smoking provide a very real deterrent to your ever considering making cigarettes a part of your life again.

Smokers in the U.S. are a small segment of a much larger group worldwide. In a typical year, smokers throughout the world will consume four and one-half trillion cigarettes.

You have also removed yourself from that group of people still being influenced by the tobacco industry. The tobacco industry in the U.S. alone spends more than $2.5 billion annually on advertising. To illustrate how strongly it wants to influence your behavior, look closely at the magazine supplement that comes with your Sunday paper. It is typically 16 to 24 pages long, with 10 to 15 percent of the pages containing cigarettes ads. These are not small ads. They are frequently full page. Aren't you glad you are no longer a smoker?

SELF-CONCEPT AND SELF-ESTEEM

It is generally accepted that, as children, our self-image is developed largely by the feedback we get from other people. The most important influences on our self-image are parents, brothers and sisters plus "significant others." This group consists of aunts, uncles, ministers, teachers, coaches, and all those who influence our becoming what we are. Their reaction to us helps us to develop a sense of WHO we are and WHAT we stand for.

You have made a major decision. You have acknowledged a habit that "controlled" you. You have looked at all the reasons you started smoking, examined all the reasons you continued smoking, and consciously determined your intention to stop smoking. You initially chose to smoke. You have now chosen to stop. You have essentially said to the world, to those who gave you the feedback you used to form your self-image in the first place:

"Thanks a lot world, I'll take it from here."

In Chapter 1, we shared a quote from Leo Buscaglia's bestselling book, "Living, Loving, and Learning." It is central enough to our theme to be repeated here.

"To hope is to risk pain. And, to try is to risk failure. But risk must be taken, because the greatest hazard in life is to risk NOTHING. The person who risks nothing does nothing, has nothing, is nothing. He may avoid suffering and sorrow, but he simply cannot learn, feel, change, grow, live, or love. Chained by his certitudes or his addictions, he's a slave. He has forfeited his greatest trait, and that is his individual freedom. Only the person who risks is free."

You had a behavior in your life you didn't like — your smoking of cigarettes. You risked "failure" when you chose the Cooper/Clayton Method. You gained "freedom" when you successfully completed the program.

121

YES, BUT WHERE DO I GO FROM HERE?

When a concerned wife, observing the 500 lb. gorilla her husband of many years led in through the back door stated, "Yes, I agree he needs a home, but where will he sleep?", her husband replied, "About anywhere he wants to, I imagine."

You would receive essentially the same response from us when you ask, "I've given up my long term addiction to nicotine — where do I go from here?" Our reply would have to be, "About anywhere you want to, we imagine."

You have mastered a very difficult challenge, you have removed an addicting drug from your life. You should feel a sense of great pride that those who are still controlled by nicotine can not even imagine.

But something equally significant has occurred. In the process of gaining control of your smoking problem, you have learned two major principles.

****

PRINCIPLE # 1.
SUCCESS IS NOTHING MORE THAN A PLAN
THAT IS ADHERED TO.

****

Let us examine how you applied that principle in your successful journey from being a smoker to being completely free of nicotine.

- You wanted or needed to become a nonsmoker.
- You became familiar with the Cooper/Clayton Method.
- You implemented the plan outlined in this book.
- You achieved your goal by adhering to the plan
- You were successful

YOU were successful. We were not successful. We simply shared the plan with you. YOU deserve the credit.

You also learned a second principle.

****

PRINCIPLE # 2
A MAJOR PROBLEM CAN BE SOLVED
WHEN CUT UP INTO A SERIES OF SMALL
PROBLEMS

****

Let us examine the past 12 to 14 weeks to see how you applied this principle.

Looking at your long term smoking pattern, considering the failures you probably experienced when you previously tried to become a non-smoker, you "observed" a major problem, a seemingly insurmountable obstacle. You cut this seemingly insurmountable obstacle into smaller and "more digestible" pieces. This is a principle that has been very effectively applied by Mary Kay Ash, the founder of Mary Kay Cosmetics, and one of the most successful business leaders in the world. She says: "You can solve any problem. You could even eat an elephant — one bite at a time."

Listed below is a summary of the way that you cut the bigger problem of how to become a nonsmoker into a series of smaller problems that didn't seem quite so big.

QUALIFICATION

1. You identified the problem as that of dealing with an addiction.

2. You determined the magnitude of the problem by recording your smoking patterns for two weeks.

REPLACEMENT AND MAINTENANCE I

1. You divided the larger problem of smoking into two problems — a drug problem (your dependence on nicotine) and the social/psychological aspects of smoking.

2. You changed the manner in which you gave your brain nicotine from the cigarette to Nicotine Replacement Therapy and reduced the amount of nicotine you used per day receiving the nicotine in a relatively steady fashion from the nicotine transdermal patch.

3. You addressed the social and psychological problems by your involvement in a comprehensive behavioral smoking-cessation program while you gave your brain nicotine at the reduced level.

ELIMINATION I AND MAINTENANCE II

1. You again reduced the amount of drug (nicotine) provided to your brain.

2. You allowed time for your brain to adjust to the reduced amount of nicotine.

3. You continued your adjustment to the social/psychological changes required to become a nonsmoker through you involvement in a comprehensive behavioral smoking-cessation program.

ELIMINATION II AND MAINTENANCE III

1. You further reduced the amount of Nicoderm® (nicotine transdermal system) each week, thus retraining your brain to accept less and less nicotine.

2. You prepared yourself to totally eliminate nicotine from your life by your involvement in a comprehensive behavioral smoking-cessation program such as the Cooper/Clayton Method.

3. You made other life-style changes to support your decision to become a nonsmoker as you continued to participate in a comprehensive behavioral smoking-cessation program.

4. You totally eliminated nicotine at the end of this period.

The most significant aspect of the total program to stop smoking is this:

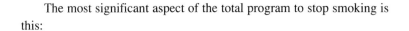

NOBODY DID IT FOR YOU.
YOU DID IT YOURSELF.

****

You initially provided nicotine to your brain. Little by little, you increased the dose. The environment at that time encouraged cigarette smoking. Smoking was associated with the "good life," "success," being "in". Many of your role models smoked cigarettes. Some prominent public figures even appeared in advertising designed to attract young people to become smokers, and to encourage those who already smoked to continue to smoke.

You have chosen to BECOME A NONSMOKER. The contemporary environment will, in all probability, become increasingly more supportive of your decision. The timing of your decision couldn't have been better. Many communities, companies, and U.S. Government agencies have passed laws and regulations severely limiting places in which smoking is allowed. One such law requires posting signs stating, "Smoking Allowed Here." How's that for a switch from the occasional "No Smoking" sign of a few years ago? The tide has turned. You managed to take control of your smoking before it was mandated that you limit your smoking rather severely. Many companies have established policies of not hiring smokers.

The almost daily coverage in public media about the harmful effects of smoking is becoming more intense. Evidence that cigarette smoking is linked to lung diseases, cardiovascular disease, numerous malignant lesions, and reduced fetal size when the mother smokes, are among the more frequently cited problems associated with cigarette smoking.

You deserve to feel good about yourself. Each time you pause and look at yourself in a mirror to comb your hair, give yourself a BIG smile, because you know something important about the person in the mirror.

You see, just as you initially taught yourself to crave nicotine, you have now taught your brain not to depend on nicotine. You have accomplished success in that area where thousands, even millions of people have been unsuccessful.

You have acquired skills that can be applied across many other aspects of your life. You have learned a secret that ALL people who are successful already knew.

****

SUCCESS IS NOT AN EVENT. IT IS A JOURNEY.

****

You have plotted your journey from being a smoker to being a nonsmoker, then taken the journey to successfully reach your chosen destination. GOOD WORK.

You have also learned a process which can assist you in achieving success in numerous other areas of life. You have come to realize that:

A journey begins with deciding where you are, proceeds to determining where you would like to be, is initiated by developing a plan to get you there, and, most importantly, is completed by following the plan.

Finally, you have learned that:

****

A journey is not really a journey, it is only a series of short trips which, collectively, add up to reaching your desired end point.

****

Now that you have mastered an addiction which controls many people for their entire life, you can master any existing or new problems that you will face.

You have skills possessed only by winners. Congratulations on your victory — your total victory over nicotine.

What else about you do you choose to change?

Remember, every journey begins with the first step.

TAKE IT!

YOU CAN DO IT!

⟞⟝◇⟞⟝

REFERENCES

1. Cooper, Thomas and Clayton, Richard: Stop Smoking Program using nicotine reduction therapy and behavior modification for heavy smokers; JADA, Vol. 118, January 1989.

2. Cooper, Thomas and Clayton, Richard: Nicotine reduction therapy and relapse prevention for heavy smokers: 3-year follow-up; JADA Supplement, January 1990.

3. Cooper, Thomas and Clayton, Richard: Behavior modification and nicotine reduction therapy with heavy smokers: Comparison of four different dosing strategies; Tobacco and Health 1990, World Conference on Tobacco and Health, April 1990 Conference Proceedings.

4. Surgeon General: The Health Consequences of Smoking: Nicotine Addiction, 1988.

5. Sachs, David P. L.: Pharmacologic, Neuroendocrine, and Biobehavioral Basis for Tobacco Dependence; Current Pulmonology, May 1987.

6. Cox, Jack and McKenna, James: Transdermal Nicotine Replacement and Smoking Cessation: American Family Physician; June, 1992.

7. Benowitz, Neal and Jacob, P.: Nicotine and carbon monoxide intake from high and low-yield cigarettes; Clinical Pharmcol Ther, 1984.

8. Benowitz, Neal: Pharmacokinetics, pharmacodynamics of nicotine differ with gum and cigarettes; Pharmacologic treatment of tobacco dependence: Proceeding of the World Congress, 1985.

9. Maslow, Abraham: Motivation and Personality; Harper and Brothers, 1954, p. 93-98.

10. Herzberg, F.: Motivation-Hygiene Profiles; Organizational Dynamics; 1974; p. 18-29.

11. Lichtenstein, E.: The smoking problem: A behavioral perspective; Journal of Consulting and Clinical Psychology, 50, 1982.

12. Ferguson, Thomas: The smoker's Book of Health; G. P. Putnam's Sons, New York, 1987.

NICORETTE®
NICORETTE®DS
(Double Strength)
(nicotine polacrilex)

DESCRIPTION

NICORETTE (nicotine polacrilex) contains nicotine bound to an ion exchange resin in a sugar-free, flavored, chewing gum base that provides systemic delivery of nicotine following chewing.

Nicotine is a tertiary amine composed of a pyridine and a pyrrolidine ring. It is a colorless to pale yellow, freely water-soluble, strongly alkaline, oily, volatile, hygroscopic liquid obtained from the tobacco plant. Nicotine has a characteristic pungent odor and turns brown on exposure to air or light. Of its two stereoisomers, S(-)nicotine is the more active. It is the prevalent form in tobacco, and is the form in the NICORETTE (nicotine polacrilex). The free alkaloid is absorbed rapidly through the skin and respiratory tract.

Chemical Name: S-3-(1-methyl-2-pyrrolidinyl) pyridine
Molecular Formula: $C_{10}H_{14}N_2$
Molecular Weight: 162.23
Ionization Constants: $pK_{a1}=7.84$, $pK_{a2}=3.04$
Octanol-Water Partition Coefficient: 15:1 at pH 7

When NICORETTE (nicotine polacrilex) is chewed as directed, nicotine is absorbed primarily through the buccal mucosa. Each piece of NICORETTE contains nicotine polacrilex equivalent to either 2 or 4 mg nicotine as the active ingredient. Each piece also contains as inactive ingredients: flavors, glycerin, gum base, sodium carbonate, and sorbitol. The 2 mg strength also contains sodium bicarbonate. The 4 mg strength also contains D&C Yellow No. 10.

Total and Extractable Nicotine Content

Nicotine Source	Nicotine Content	Nicotine Extracted
NICORETTE DS	4 mg/piece	3.4 mg[a]
NICORETTE	2 mg/piece	1.4 mg[a]
American Cigarettes	11 mg/cigarette	0.8 mg[b]

[a] Extracted with paced chewing once every other second for 30 minutes (more vigorous than recommended use, see PATIENT INSTRUCTIONS).
[b] Nicotine extracted *in vitro* by smoking machine.

CLINICAL PHARMACOLOGY
Pharmacologic Action

Nicotine, the chief alkaloid in tobacco products, binds stereoselectively to acetylcholine receptors at the autonomic ganglia, in the adrenal medulla, at neuromuscular junctions, and in the brain. Two types of central nervous system effects are believed to be the basis of nicotine's positively reinforcing properties. A stimulating effect, exerted mainly in the cortex via the locus ceruleus, produces increased alertness and cognitive performance. A "reward" effect via the "pleasure system" in the brain is exerted in the limbic system. At low doses the stimulant effects predominate while at high doses the reward effects predominate. Intermittent intravenous administration of nicotine activates neurohormonal pathways, releasing acetylcholine, norepinephrine, dopamine, serotonin, vasopressin, beta-endorphin, growth hormone, and ACTH.

Pharmacodynamics

The cardiovascular effects of nicotine include peripheral vasoconstriction, tachycardia, and elevated blood pressure. Acute and chronic tolerance to nicotine develops from smoking tobacco or ingesting nicotine preparations. Acute tolerance (a reduction in response for a given dose) develops rapidly (less than 1 hour), however, not at the same rate for different physiologic effects (skin temperature, heart rate, subjective effects).

Withdrawal symptoms such as cigarette craving can be reduced in some individuals by plasma nicotine levels lower than those from smoking.

Withdrawal from nicotine in addicted individuals is characterized by craving, nervousness, restlessness, irritability, mood lability, anxiety, drowsiness, sleep disturbances, impaired concentration, increased appetite, minor somatic complaints (headache, myalgia, constipation, fatigue), and weight gain. Nicotine toxicity is characterized by nausea, abdominal pain, vomiting, diarrhea, diaphoresis, flushing, dizziness, disturbed hearing and vision, confusion, weakness, palpitations, altered respirations and hypotension.

Both smoking and nicotine can increase circulating cortisol and catecholamines, and tolerance does not develop to the catecholamine-releasing effects of nicotine. Changes in the response to a concomitantly administered adrenergic agonist or antagonist should be watched for when nicotine intake is altered during NICORETTE therapy and/or smoking cessation (see PRECAUTIONS: Drug Interactions).

Pharmacokinetics

The volume of distribution following IV administration of nicotine is approximately 2 to 3 L/kg and the half-life ranges from 1 to 2 hours. The major eliminating organ is the liver, and average plasma clearance is about 1.2 L/min; the kidney and lung also metabolize nicotine. More than 20 metabolites of nicotine have been identified, all of which are believed to be less active than the parent compound. The primary metabolite of nicotine in plasma, cotinine, has a half-life of 15 to 20 hours and concentrations that exceed nicotine by 10-fold.

Plasma protein binding of nicotine is < 5%. Therefore, changes in nicotine binding from use of concomitant drugs or alterations of plasma proteins by disease states would not be expected to have significant effect on nicotine kinetics.

The primary urinary metabolites are cotinine (15% of the dose) and trans-3-hydroxycotinine (45% of the dose). Usually about 10% of nicotine is excreted unchanged in the urine. As much as 30% may be excreted unchanged in the urine with high urine flow rates and acidification below pH 5.

The amount of nicotine extracted from a NICORETTE chewing piece depends on how vigorously it is chewed. The amount of nicotine absorbed depends on the amount extracted and the loss from the buccal cavity due to swallowing or expectoration. Most of the absorption of nicotine from a NICORETTE chewing piece occurs directly through the buccal mucosa. The systemic bioavailability of swallowed nicotine is lower due to the amount removed initially by the liver, i.e., the first pass effect. Hence, the high and rapidly rising nicotine concentrations seen after smoking are rarely produced by NICORETTE treatment.

The table below presents results from a bioavailability study in which 24 smokers chewed a single NICORETTE chewing piece at a vigorous, prescribed rate. The values in this table thus represent maximum plasma nicotine levels (higher than expected upon normal use and recommended chewing).

Bioavailability of Single 2 and 4 mg Doses
(N = 24 smokers, vigorous paced chewing)

Labeled Dose (mg)	Number (N)	Extracted Amount (mg)*[a]	Systemically Available Amount (mg)*[b]
4	16	3.4 (3.1-3.7)	2.5 (1.8-3.2)
2	18	1.4 (1.1-1.6)	1.3 (0.6-1.9)

* Mean, 95% confidence interval.

[a] determined by measuring amount in the chewing pieces before and after 30 minutes of paced chewing.
[b] determined by measuring amount in plasma (area under the curve) during and after 30 minutes of paced chewing.

Acidic beverages (e.g., coffee, juices, wine or soft drinks), interfere with the buccal absorption of nicotine from NICORETTE (nicotine polacrilex). Eating and drinking should therefore be avoided for 15 minutes before and during chewing of NICORETTE.

Nicotine Concentrations in Plasma While Smoking ad lib (N=14) and Chewing 12 pieces/day of NICORETTE (N=7) (Mean ±2 SD)

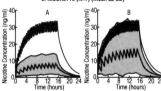

The figure shows simulated nicotine venous plasma concentrations after multiple dosing of NICORETTE 2 mg/piece (plot A), NICORETTE DS 4 mg/piece (plot B) and cigarette smoking (shaded area represents +/-SD for the nicotine polacrilex products). The dosing regimens and absorbed amounts of nicotine are idealized from data reported by Benowitz, et al. (Clin Pharmacol Ther 1987; 41:467-473). When a single piece was chewed slowly and steadily for 20 minutes every 1.3 hours for 16 hours (12 pieces total); 0.85 and 1.22 mg nicotine was absorbed on average from NICORETTE and NICORETTE DS, respectively. An average of thirty-eight cigarettes of these volunteers' own brand, delivering an average of 1 mg nicotine each were smoked ad lib over the same time period.

CLINICAL STUDIES

The efficacy of NICORETTE treatment as an aid to smoking cessation was demonstrated in four placebo-controlled, double-blind trials in otherwise healthy patients. Two of the trials involved only the 2 mg dose and two used both 2 and 4 mg doses. Quitting was defined as total abstinence from smoking for 4 weeks as measured by patient diary and verified by expired carbon monoxide after an initial two weeks of treatment. The "quit rates" are the proportions of all persons initially enrolled who abstained Weeks 2-6.

The two trials using both 2 mg (NICORETTE) and 4 mg (NICORETTE DS) doses in otherwise healthy smokers with concomitant support (N=563) showed that NICORETTE treatment was more effective than placebo after 6 weeks in the patients (N=289) using more than 9 pieces per day. These results emphasize the importance of adequate nicotine doses. The quit rates among clinics varied approximately 2 to 3-fold for each treatment (see table).

Quit Rate After Week 2 By Starting Dose
(N=563 smokers in 6 clinics)

NICORETTE Dose (mg/piece)	All patients Enrolled		Patients using > 9 pcs/dy	
	Number of Patients	After 6 weeks (range)*	Number of Patients	After 6 weeks (range)+
4	189	17-59%	93	29-74%
2	190	21-47%	104	10-54%
Placebo	184	23-39%	92	20-44%

* Range for 6 clinics, number of patients per treatment ranged from 29-37.
+ Range for 6 clinics, number of patients per treatment ranged from 7-23.

Patients who used NICORETTE DS (nicotine polacrilex) in clinical trials had a significant reduction in craving for cigarettes, a major nicotine withdrawal symptom, as compared to placebo-treated patients. Reduction in craving, as with quit rate, is quite variable. This variability is presumed to be due to inherent differences in patient populations, e.g., patient motivation, concomitant illnesses, number of cigarettes smoked per day, number of years smoking, exposure to other smokers, socioeconomic status, etc., as well as differences among the clinics.

Patients using NICORETTE treatment dropped out of the clinical trials less frequently than did patients using placebo.

Individualization of Dosage

It is important to make sure that patients read the instructions made available to them and have their questions answered. They should clearly understand the directions for using and disposing of NICORETTE (nicotine polacrilex). They should be instructed to stop smoking completely when the first NICORETTE dose is used.

The success or failure of smoking cessation depends heavily on the quality, intensity and frequency of supportive care. Patients are more likely to quit smoking if they are seen frequently and participate in formal smoking cessation programs.

The goal of NICORETTE therapy is complete abstinence. Significant health benefits have not been demonstrated for reduction of smoking. If a patient is unable to stop smoking by the fourth week of therapy, treatment should probably be discontinued. Patients who have not stopped smoking after 4 weeks of NICORETTE therapy are unlikely to quit on that attempt.

Patients who fail to quit on any attempt may benefit from interventions to improve their chances for success on subsequent attempts. Patients who were unsuccessful should be counseled to determine why they failed. Patients should then probably be given a "therapy holiday" before the next attempt. A new quit attempt should be encouraged when the factors that contributed to failure can be eliminated or reduced, and conditions are more favorable.

Based on the clinical trials, a reasonable approach to assisting patients in their attempt to quit smoking is to assign their initial NICORETTE dose based on the severity of their dependence (see Fagerstrom Tolerance Questionnaire below). The need for dose adjustment should be assessed during the first 2 weeks. Patients should continue the dose selected with concomitant support and periodic evaluation. Those who have successfully stopped smoking during that time should be supported during 1 to 3 months of weaning, after which treatment should be terminated.

Therapy should generally begin with the NICORETTE DS (4-mg dose) in individuals who score ≥ 7 on the Fagerstrom Tolerance Questionnaire (FTQ) or who are determined to be highly dependent by some other measure (consumption of > 25 cigarettes/day, carbon monoxide, cotinine, et al).

The Fagerstrom Tolerance Questionnaire

Questions	Answers	Points
1. How soon after you wake up do you smoke your first cigarette?	Within 30 min. After 30 min.	1 0
2. Do you find it difficult to refrain from smoking in places where it is forbidden; e.g., in church, library, cinemas, etc?	Yes No	1 0
3. Which cigarette would you hate the most to give up?	The first one in the morning Any other	1 0
4. How many cigarettes a day do you smoke?	≤ 15 16-25 ≥ 26	0 1 2
5. Do you smoke more frequently during the hours after awakening than during the rest of the day?	Yes No	1 0
6. Do you smoke if you are so ill that you are in bed most of the day?	Yes No	1 0
7. What is the nicotine level of your usual brand of cigarette?	≤ 0.6 mg 0.61-1.0 mg > 1.0 mg	0 1 2
8. Do you inhale?	Never Sometimes Always	0 1 2

Total 0-11. Highly nicotine dependent smokers ≥ 7 points.

The symptoms of nicotine withdrawal and excess overlap (see CLINICAL PHARMACOLOGY and ADVERSE REACTIONS sections). Since patients using NICORETTE treatment might also smoke intermittently, it may be difficult to determine if patients are experiencing nicotine withdrawal or nicotine excess.

The controlled clinical trials comparing NICORETTE (2-mg), NICORETTE DS (4-mg) and placebo doses suggest that dyspepsia and nausea are more often symptoms of nicotine excess while flatulence and depression are more often symptoms of nicotine withdrawal.

In a 24-month study where, all subjects were provided access to 2 mg NICORETTE pieces after the 6 week double-blind phase, 54% used the product after 3 months, 16% after 6 months, 6% after 12 months, and 3% after 24 months. To minimize the risk of dependence, patients should be encouraged to withdraw gradually from NICORETTE treatment after 2 to 3 months of use (see DOSAGE AND ADMINISTRATION).

INDICATIONS AND USAGE

NICORETTE treatment is indicated as an aid to smoking cessation for the relief of nicotine withdrawal symptoms. NICORETTE treatment should be used as a part of a comprehensive behavioral smoking cessation program.

The use of NICORETTE (nicotine polacrilex) for longer than 6 months has not been adequately studied.

CONTRAINDICATIONS

Use of NICORETTE (nicotine polacrilex) is contraindicated in patients with hypersensitivity or allergy to nicotine or to any of the components of NICORETTE (nicotine polacrilex).

WARNINGS

Nicotine from any source can be toxic and addictive. Smoking causes lung cancer, heart disease, emphysema, and may adversely affect the fetus and the pregnant woman. For any smoker, with or without concomitant disease or pregnancy, the risk of nicotine replacement in a smoking cessation program should be weighed against the hazard of continued smoking during NICORETTE treatment, and the likelihood of achieving cessation of smoking without nicotine replacement.

Pregnancy Warning

Tobacco smoke, which has been shown to be harmful to the fetus, contains nicotine, hydrogen cyanide, and carbon monoxide. Nicotine has been shown in animal studies to cause fetal harm. It is therefore presumed that NICORETTE (nicotine polacrilex) treatment can cause fetal harm when administered to a pregnant woman. The effect of nicotine delivery by NICORETTE (nicotine polacrilex) has been examined in single dose trials in pregnancy and shown to have less fetal cardiovascular effect than cigarette smoking (see PRECAUTIONS).

Pregnant smokers should be encouraged to attempt cessation using educational and behavioral interventions, however, before using pharmacological approaches. If NICORETTE (nicotine polacrilex) therapy is used during pregnancy, or if the patient becomes pregnant while using NICORETTE (nicotine polacrilex), the patient should be apprised of the potential hazard to the fetus.

Safety Note Concerning Children

The amounts of nicotine that are tolerated by adult smokers can produce symptoms of poisoning and could prove fatal if NICORETTE (nicotine polacrilex) is chewed or ingested by children or pets. Following recommended use, NICORETTE chewing pieces contain about 50% of their initial drug content. Therefore, patients should be cautioned to keep both used and unused NICORETTE out of the reach of children and pets.

130

PRECAUTIONS
The patient should be urged to stop smoking completely when initiating NICORETTE therapy (see DOSAGE AND ADMINISTRATION). Patients should be informed that if they continue to smoke while using NICORETTE (nicotine polacrilex), they may experience adverse effects due to peak nicotine levels higher than those experienced from smoking alone. If there is a clinically significant increase in cardiovascular or other effects attributable to nicotine, the NICORETTE dose should be reduced or treatment discontinued (see WARNINGS). Physicians should anticipate that concomitant medications may need dosage adjustment (see PRECAUTIONS: Drug Interactions).

The sustained use of NICORETTE (nicotine polacrilex) by patients who stop smoking should be discouraged because the chronic consumption of nicotine by any route can be harmful and addicting.

Allergic Reactions
Allergic reactions to NICORETTE (nicotine polacrilex) have been reported in post-marketing surveillance. Patients with allergic reactions to NICORETTE (nicotine polacrilex) should be cautioned that a serious reaction could occur from exposure to other nicotine-containing products or smoking.

Patients should be instructed to discontinue the use of NICORETTE (nicotine polacrilex) promptly and contact their physician in the case of severe reactions (e.g., urticaria, hives or generalized rashes).

Oral/Pharyngeal Conditions
Use with caution in patients with oral or pharyngeal inflammation or a history of esophagitis.

NICORETTE (nicotine polacrilex) has been formulated to minimize its stickiness. As with other chewing gums, it may still adhere to dentures, dental caps, or partial bridges. Patients should be made aware of this, and should be instructed to discontinue use of NICORETTE chewing pieces if stickiness to dental work becomes a problem (see PATIENT INSTRUCTIONS).

Cardiovascular or Peripheral Vascular Diseases
The risks of nicotine replacement in patients with certain cardiovascular and peripheral vascular diseases should be weighed against the benefits of including nicotine replacement in a smoking cessation program for them. Specifically, patients with coronary heart disease (history of myocardial infarction and/or angina pectoris), serious cardiac arrhythmias, or vasospastic diseases (Buerger's disease, Prinzmetal's variant angina) should be carefully screened and evaluated before nicotine replacement is prescribed.

Cardiovascular events occurring in association with the use of NICORETTE (nicotine polacrilex) have been reported (see ADVERSE REACTIONS). In post-marketing surveillance of NICORETTE 2 mg in the US, several deaths have been reported including congestive heart failure, myocardial infarction, cardiac arrest, and cerebrovascular accident. A cause and effect between these events and the use of NICORETTE (nicotine polacrilex) has not been established. If serious cardiovascular symptoms occur with NICORETTE therapy, it should be discontinued.

NICORETTE (nicotine polacrilex) should generally not be used in patients during the immediate post-myocardial infarction period, patients with serious arrhythmias, and patients with severe or worsening angina pectoris.

Renal or Hepatic Insufficiency
The pharmacokinetics of nicotine have not been studied in the elderly or patients with renal or hepatic impairment. However, given that nicotine is extensively metabolized and that its total systemic clearance is dependent on liver blood flow, some influence of hepatic impairment on drug kinetics (reduced clearance) should be anticipated. Only severe renal impairment would be expected to affect the clearance of nicotine or its metabolites from the circulation (see CLINICAL PHARMACOLOGY: Pharmacokinetics).

Endocrine Diseases
NICORETTE treatment should be used with caution in patients with hyperthyroidism, pheochromocytoma or insulin-dependent diabetes since nicotine causes the release of catecholamines by the adrenal medulla.

Peptic Ulcer Disease
Nicotine delays healing in peptic ulcer disease; therefore NICORETTE treatment should be used with caution in patients with active peptic ulcers and only when the benefits of including nicotine replacement in a smoking cessation program outweigh the risks.

Accelerated Hypertension
Nicotine constitutes a risk factor for development of malignant hypertension in patients with accelerated hypertension; therefore NICORETTE treatment should be used with caution in these patients and only when the benefits of including nicotine replacement in a smoking cessation program outweigh the risks.

Information for Patient
A patient instruction sheet is included in the package of NICORETTE (nicotine polacrilex) dispensed to the patient. It contains important information and instructions on how to properly use and dispose of NICORETTE chewing pieces. Patients should be encouraged to ask questions of the physician and pharmacist.

Patients must be advised to keep both used and unused NICORETTE (nicotine polacrilex) out of the reach of children and pets.

Drug Interactions
Smoking cessation, with or without nicotine replacement, may alter the pharmacokinetics of certain concomitant medications.

May Require a Decrease in Dose at Cessation of Smoking	Possible Mechanism
acetaminophen, caffeine, imipramine, oxazepam, pentazocine, propranolol, theophylline	Deinduction of hepatic enzymes on smoking cessation.
insulin	Increase of subcutaneous insulin absorption with smoking cessation.
adrenergic antagonists (e.g., prazosin, labetalol)	Decrease in circulating catecholamines with smoking cessation.

May Require an Increase in Dose at Cessation of Smoking	Possible Mechanism
adrenergic agonists (e.g., isoproterenol, phenylephrine)	Decrease in circulating catecholamines with smoking cessation.

Carcinogenesis, Mutagenesis, Impairment of Fertility
Nicotine itself does not appear to be a carcinogen in laboratory animals. However, nicotine and its metabolites increased the incidences of tumors in the cheek pouches of hamsters and forestomachs of F344 rats, when given in combination with tumor-initiators. One study, which could not be replicated, suggested that cotinine, the primary metabolite of nicotine, may cause lymphoreticular sarcoma in the large intestine in rats.

Nicotine and cotinine were not mutagenic in the Ames' *Salmonella* test. Nicotine induced repairable DNA damage in an *E. coli* test system. Nicotine was shown to be genotoxic in a test system using Chinese hamster ovary cells. In rats and rabbits, implantation can be delayed or inhibited by a reduction in DNA synthesis that appears to be caused by nicotine. Studies have shown a decrease in litter size in rats treated with nicotine during gestation.

Pregnancy
Pregnancy Category C (see WARNINGS section).
The harmful effects of cigarette smoking on maternal and fetal health are clearly established. These include low birth weight, an increased risk of spontaneous abortion, and increased perinatal mortality. Nicotine produced skeletal abnormalities in the offspring of pregnant mice who received toxic doses (25 mg/kg IP or SC, 700 x the 2.5 mg dose absorbed systemically from a single NICORETTE DS) in one study. Nicotine, 1.67 mg/kg/day IP on days 6-15 of gestation, caused decreased crown-rump length, fetal weight and head size and increased rate of cleft palate in the offspring of pregnant mice. There are no adequate and well-controlled multiple dose studies in pregnant women. Therefore pregnant smokers should be encouraged to attempt cessation using educational and behavioral interventions before using pharmacological approaches. Spontaneous abortion during nicotine replacement therapy has been reported; as with smoking, nicotine as a contributing factor cannot be excluded.

NICORETTE (nicotine polacrilex) treatment should be used during pregnancy only if the potential benefit considering the likelihood of smoking cessation justifies the potential risk to the fetus of using NICORETTE (nicotine polacrilex) by the patient, who might continue to smoke.

Human studies
Smoking: Cigarette smoking during pregnancy is associated with an increased risk of spontaneous abortion, low birth weight infants and perinatal mortality. Current thought implicates nicotine and carbon monoxide as the most likely mediators of these outcomes.

Nicotine: The effect of nicotine, administered as 2 and 4 mg nicotine gum and cigarette smoking, on fetal cardiovascular parameters has been studied near term. One or two cigarettes increased fetal aortic blood flow and heart rate, and decreased uterine blood flow and fetal breathing movement. One or two pieces of 2 or 4 mg gum (delivering 1 to 4 mg of nicotine) had less effect on these parameters.

Teratogenicity
Animal Studies: Nicotine was shown to produce skeletal abnormalities, cleft palate, and other effects in mice (see PREGNANCY).

Human Studies: Nicotine teratogenicity has not been studied in humans except as a component of cigarette smoke (each cigarette smoked delivers about 1 mg of nicotine). It has not been possible to conclude whether cigarette smoking is teratogenic to humans.

Other Effects
Animal Studies: A nicotine bolus (up to 2 mg/kg) to pregnant rhesus monkeys caused acidosis, hypercarbia, and hypotension (fetal and maternal concentrations were about 20 times those achieved after smoking one cigarette in 5 minutes). Fetal breathing movements were reduced in the fetal lamb after intravenous injection of 0.25 mg/kg nicotine to the ewe (equivalent to smoking one cigarette every 20 seconds for 5 minutes). Uterine blood flow was reduced about 30% after infusion of 2 mg/kg nicotine over 20 min to pregnant rhesus monkeys (equivalent to smoking about 120 cigarettes over 20 minutes).

Labor and Delivery
NICORETTE treatment is not recommended during labor and delivery. The effects of nicotine on the mother or the fetus during labor are unknown.

Use in Nursing Mothers

Caution should be exercised when NICORETTE (nicotine polacrilex) is administered to nursing women. The safety of NICORETTE treatment in nursing infants has not been examined. Nicotine passes freely into breast milk; the milk to plasma ratio averages 2.9. Nicotine is absorbed orally. An infant has the ability to clear nicotine by hepatic first pass clearance, however the efficiency of removal is probably lowest at birth. The nicotine concentrations in breast milk can be expected to be lower with NICORETTE treatment when used as directed than with cigarette smoking, as maternal plasma nicotine concentrations are generally reduced with nicotine replacement. The risk of exposure of the infant to nicotine from NICORETTE treatment should be weighed against the risks associated with the infant's exposure to nicotine from continued smoking by the mother (passive smoke exposure and contamination of breast milk with other components of tobacco smoke) or from NICORETTE therapy in combination with continued smoking.

Pediatric Use

NICORETTE treatment is not recommended for use in children because the safety and effectiveness of NICORETTE treatment in children and adolescents who smoke have not been evaluated.

Geriatric Use

Review of post-marketing data with NICORETTE 2 mg nicotine polacrilex does not reveal age-related trends in either incidence of character or adverse events.

ADVERSE REACTIONS

Assessment of adverse events in the 519 patients who participated in clinical trials of both 2 mg and 4 mg NICORETTE doses is complicated by the occurrence of GI and CNS effects of nicotine withdrawal as well as nicotine excess. The actual incidences of both are confounded by concurrent smoking by many of the patients. In the trials, when reporting adverse events, the investigators did not attempt to identify the cause of the symptom.

Oral Adverse Events

Oral adverse events occurring with a frequency of 1% or greater among 174 patients using NICORETTE DS in clinical trials involving 519 patients were stomatitis (excluding aphthous and ulcerative stomatitis) 5%, aphthous stomatitis 5%, tooth disorder 4%, glossitis 3%, gingival bleeding 1%, tongue ulceration 1%, and ulcerative stomatitis 1%.

Probably Causally Related

The following adverse events were reported more frequently in NICORETTE-treated patients than in placebo-treated patients or exhibited a dose response in clinical trials.

Digestive System — Diarrhea[+], dyspepsia (12%), hiccup[*], nausea (10%), salivation increased[*].

Mouth/Tooth Disorders — Dry mouth[+].
Musculoskeletal — Myalgia[*].
Nervous System — paraesthesia[*].
Skin and Appendages — Sweating[+].

Frequencies for NICORETTE DS
[*] Reported in 3% to 9% of patients.
[+] Reported in 1% to 3% of patients.
Unmarked if reported in < 1% of patients.

Causal relationship UNKNOWN

Adverse events reported in NICORETTE- and placebo-treated patients at about the same frequency in clinical trials are listed below. Selected events from post-marketing surveillance of NICORETTE 2 mg treatment are also included. The clinical significance of the association between NICORETTE treatment and these events is unknown, but they are reported as alerting information for the clinician.

Body as a whole — Allergy[*], back pain[*], chest pain[+], pain[*], *erythema, pruritus.*
Cardiovascular system — Hypertension[+], *edema, flushing, palpitations, tachyarrhythmias, tachycardia.*
Digestive system — Abdominal pain[*], *anorexia, alteration of liver function tests,* constipation[*], eructation[*], flatulence[+], vomiting[+].
Mouth/tooth disorder — Aphthous stomatitis[*], *gingivitis, glossitis[+], jaw pain,* stomatitis[*], *taste perception changes,* tooth disorder[*].
Nervous system — Concentration impaired[*], *confusion, convulsions, depression,* dizziness[*], *euphoria,* headache (20%), *insomnia[*], irritability, tinnitus.*
Respiratory system — *Breathing difficulty,* congestion[*], cough increased[*], *hoarseness,* throat irritation[*], *wheezing.*
Urogenital System — Dysmenorrhea[*].

Frequencies for NICORETTE DS
[*] Reported in 3% to 9% of patients.
[+] Reported in 1% to 3% of patients.
Unmarked if reported in < 1% of patients.
Italics indicate reports from post-marketing surveillance of NICORETTE (nicotine polacrilex) 2 mg.

DRUG ABUSE AND DEPENDENCE

NICORETTE (nicotine polacrilex) is likely to have a low abuse potential based on differences between it and cigarettes in four characteristics commonly considered important in contributing to abuse: slower absorption, smaller fluctuations in blood levels, lower blood levels of nicotine, and less frequent use (9-12 pieces/day).

Dependence on NICORETTE replacement therapy has been reported. Such dependence may represent transference to NICORETTE (nicotine polacrilex) of tobacco-based nicotine dependence. The use of NICORETTE treatment beyond 6 months has not been evaluated in well-controlled studies and should be discouraged.

To minimize the risk of dependence, patients should be encouraged to withdraw gradually from NICORETTE therapy after 2 to 3 months of usage. Recommended dose reduction is to progressively decrease the dose every 4 to 7 days (see DOSAGE AND ADMINISTRATION).

OVERDOSAGE

Overdosage can occur if many pieces are chewed simultaneously or in rapid succession. The polacrilex resin requires chewing to release the nicotine and limits nicotine release from swallowed gum.

The oral LD$_{50}$ for nicotine in rodents varies with species but is in excess of 24 mg/kg; death is due to respiratory paralysis. The oral minimum lethal dose of nicotine in dogs is greater than 5 mg/kg. The oral minimum acute lethal dose for nicotine in human adults is reported to be 40 to 60 mg (< 1 mg/kg).

Signs and symptoms of an overdose of NICORETTE (nicotine polacrilex) would be expected to be the same as those of acute nicotine poisoning including: pallor, cold sweat, nausea, salivation, vomiting, abdominal pain, diarrhea, headache, dizziness, disturbed hearing and vision, tremor, mental confusion, and weakness. Prostration, hypotension, and respiratory failure may ensue with large overdoses. Lethal doses produce convulsions quickly and death follows as a result of peripheral or central respiratory paralysis or, less frequently, cardiac failure.

Overdose from Ingestion

Review of reported overdoses in children ranging from 20 months to 9 years of age who had chewed or swallowed 1/2 - 4 pieces of 2 mg NICORETTE (nicotine polacrilex) revealed no fatalities. Symptoms reported include nausea, vomiting, lethargy, abdominal pain, hypotension, agitation and tachycardia. All symptoms resolved within 24 hours with only supportive treatment and observation. Used NICORETTE pieces may contain about 50% of their initial drug content. Therefore, patients should be cautioned to keep both the used and unused NICORETTE pieces out of the reach of children and pets.

Due to the slow release of nicotine from the polacrilex resin, activated charcoal alone may be adequate for most ingestions. In unconscious patients with a secure airway, instill activated charcoal. A saline cathartic or sorbitol added to the first dose of activated charcoal may speed gastrointestinal passage of the gum.

Management of Nicotine Poisoning

Other supportive measures include diazepam or barbiturates for seizures, atropine for excessive bronchial secretions or diarrhea, respiratory support for respiratory failure, and vigorous fluid support for hypotension and cardiovascular collapse.

DOSAGE AND ADMINISTRATION

Patients must desire to stop smoking and should be instructed to *stop smoking immediately.* The patient should read the patient instruction sheet on NICORETTE treatment and be encouraged to ask any questions.

The initial dosage of NICORETTE should be individualized on the basis of each patient's nicotine dependence. Highly dependent smokers (Fagerstrom Tolerance Score ≥ 7, or > 25 cigarettes/day) should receive the 4 mg dose, initially. Other patients should begin treatment with the 2 mg dosage strength. Increasing to the 4 mg dose may be considered for patients who fail to stop smoking with the 2 mg dose, or for those whose nicotine withdrawal symptoms remain so strong as to threaten relapse.

Recommended Dosing Schedule for Healthy Patients

Dose	Patient dependency (FTQ)	Number of pieces to be used per day	Maximum pieces per day
NICORETTE DS	≥ 7	9-12	20
NICORETTE 2 mg	< 7	9-12	30

It is important for the patients to learn to chew NICORETTE (nicotine polacrilex) slowly and to self-titrate the nicotine dose, in order to minimize side effects (see PATIENT INSTRUCTIONS Sheet at the end of product labeling).

Each piece of NICORETTE should be chewed intermittently for about 30 minutes. The aim of this chewing procedure is to promote slow buccal absorption of the nicotine released from NICORETTE. Chewing too quickly can rapidly release the nicotine which leads to effects similar to oversmoking: nausea, hiccups, or irritation of the throat. Since nicotine is poorly absorbed from the stomach, swallowed nicotine may contribute to gastrointestinal adverse effects without relieving withdrawal. Proper chewing technique (slow paced chewing and intermittent parking) is designed to minimize swallowed nicotine.

Acidic beverages (e.g., coffee, juices, wine or soft drinks), interfere with the buccal absorption of nicotine from NICORETTE (nicotine polacrilex). Eating and drinking should therefore be avoided for 15 minutes before and during chewing of NICORETTE.

Clinical experience suggests that abstinence (quit) rates may be higher when patients chew NICORETTE on a fixed schedule (one piece every 1 to 2 hours) than when allowed to chew it *ad libitum.*

Patients using the 2 mg strength should not exceed 30 pieces per day, whereas those using the 4 mg strength should not exceed 20 pieces per day.

When used for smoking cessation, gradual weaning from NICORETTE treatment should be initiated after 2 to 3 months and completed by 4 to 6 months. Some ex-smokers may need NICORETTE treatment longer to avoid returning to smoking.

Gradual Reduction Procedures for Use in Smoking Cessation
Gradual withdrawal of NICORETTE treatment should be initiated to avoid the recurrence of symptoms which may lead to a return to smoking. Suggested procedures for gradually reducing NICORETTE dosage include:

1. Decrease the total number of pieces of NICORETTE used per day by one or more pieces every 4 to 7 days.

2. Decrease the chewing time with each piece of NICORETTE from the normal 30 minutes to 10 to 15 minutes for 4 to 7 days. Then gradually decrease the total number of pieces used per day.

3. Others may want to chew each piece for longer than 30 minutes and reduce the number of pieces used per day.

4. Substitute one or more pieces of sugarless gum for an equal number of pieces of NICORETTE. Increase the number of pieces of sugarless gum substituted for NICORETTE chewing pieces every 4 to 7 days.

5. Replace NICORETTE 4 mg with 2 mg and apply any of the above suggested procedures.

Withdrawal of NICORETTE treatment may be individualized by modifying or combining the above procedures. NICORETTE treatment may be stopped when usage has been reduced to one or two pieces per day.

SAFETY AND HANDLING
NICORETTE (nicotine polacrilex) is dispensed in individual blister packages which pose no known risk to health care workers if given, unopened to the patient.

Disposal
Used NICORETTE chewing pieces should be placed in a wrapper and disposed of in such a way to prevent its access by children or pets. See patient information for further directions for handling and disposal.

HOW SUPPLIED
NDC 0068-0045-55
    NICORETTE 2 mg (beige) square chewing pieces.

NDC 0068-0047-55
    NICORETTE DS (yellow) square chewing pieces.

Each strength is packaged in child-resistant blister strips of 12 chewing pieces per strip, 8 strips per box, i.e., 96 chewing pieces per box.

HOW TO STORE
Do not store above 86°F (30°C) because the nicotine in NICORETTE (nicotine polacrilex) is sensitive to heat. Protect from light.

Do not store out of the blister. Once removed from the protective pack, NICORETTE (nicotine polacrilex) should be used promptly since nicotine is volatile and it may lose strength.

CAUTION: Federal law prohibits dispensing without prescription.

Manufactured by
Kabi Pharmacia AB, Uppsala, Sweden for
Merrell Dow Pharmaceuticals Inc.
Subsidiary of
Marion Merrell Dow Inc.
Kansas City, MO 64114

Product Information as of November 1992   J172N

NICORETTE®
2 mg

NICORETTE®DS
(Double Strength) 4mg
(nicotine polacrilex)

IMPORTANT

YOUR DOCTOR HAS PRESCRIBED NICORETTE CHEWING PIECES FOR YOUR USE ONLY. DO NOT LET ANYONE ELSE USE IT.

KEEP NICORETTE CHEWING PIECES OUT OF REACH OF CHILDREN AND PETS. Nicotine can be harmful. Small amounts of nicotine can cause serious illness in children. Even used NICORETTE chewing pieces contain nicotine. Be sure to throw used pieces away out of the reach of children and pets. **If a child chews or swallows one or more pieces of NICORETTE, contact a poison control center, or contact your doctor immediately.**

Women: Nicotine in any form may cause harm to your unborn baby if you use nicotine while you are pregnant. Do not use NICORETTE if you are pregnant or breast feeding unless advised by your doctor. If you become pregnant while using or if you think you might be pregnant, stop smoking and don't use NICORETTE chewing pieces until you have talked to your doctor.

This leaflet will provide you with general information about nicotine and specific instruction about how to use NICORETTE chewing pieces. It is important that you read it carefully and completely before you start using NICORETTE. Be sure to read the PRECAUTIONS section before using NICORETTE chewing pieces, because, as with all drugs, NICORETTE treatment has side effects. Since this leaflet is only a summary of information, be sure to ask your doctor if you have any questions or want to know more.

INTRODUCTION

IT IS IMPORTANT THAT YOU ARE FIRMLY COMMITTED TO GIVING UP SMOKING.

While using NICORETTE, you are more likely to successfully quit smoking if you see your doctor regularly for encouragement and/or participate in an organized smoking cessation program. Ask your doctor which kind of program would be best for you.

NICORETTE chewing pieces contain nicotine in a gum base and are designed to help you quit smoking cigarettes. The correct use of this medicine is different from chewing gums. While you are chewing NICORETTE, it releases nicotine into your bloodstream through the lining of your mouth.

It is the nicotine in cigarettes that causes addiction to smoking. NICORETTE chewing pieces replace some of the nicotine you crave while you are stopping smoking.

NICORETTE treatment may also help relieve other symptoms that may occur when you stop smoking.

There are two doses of NICORETTE chewing pieces. Your doctor has chosen the dose of NICORETTE you are using. After 2 to 3 months, your doctor will have you use fewer pieces of NICORETTE. In time, you should not need any nicotine.

INFORMATION ABOUT NICORETTE CHEWING PIECES

How NICORETTE Chewing Pieces Work

NICORETTE chewing pieces contain nicotine. When you use NICORETTE chewing pieces correctly, nicotine passes from the chewed piece through the lining of your mouth and into your blood.

HOW TO USE NICORETTE CHEWING PIECES

READ **ALL** OF THE FOLLOWING STEPS BEFORE USING NICORETTE CHEWING PIECES.

REFER TO THESE INSTRUCTIONS OFTEN TO MAKE SURE YOU ARE USING NICORETTE CHEWING PIECES CORRECTLY.

1) If you want to stop, you must give up smoking completely, starting now.

2) To prevent craving and other withdrawal symptoms, take one piece of NICORETTE every 1-2 hours or as directed by your physician.

3) Chew NICORETTE chewing pieces very slowly.

4) Stop chewing when you have a peppery taste or feel a slight tingling in your mouth.
   (This happens after about 15 chews. The number of chews is not the same for all people).

5) "Park" the gum.
   To "park" the gum, place it between the cheek and gums.

6) Start to chew slowly again when the taste or tingling is almost gone (about 1 minute).
   When the peppery taste or tingling returns, stop chewing.

7) "Park" the gum again in a different part of the mouth.

8) Repeat steps 3 through 7 until most of the nicotine is gone from the gum (about 30 minutes).

9) Dispose of the used NICORETTE chewing pieces in the trash away from children and pets.

DO NOT USE MORE THAN 20 PIECES OF NICORETTE DS OR 30 PIECES OF NICORETTE 2 MG A DAY.

MOST PEOPLE FIND THAT 9 TO 12 PIECES OF NICORETTE DS A DAY WILL CONTROL THEIR URGE TO SMOKE.

DO NOT USE NICORETTE CHEWING PIECES FOR MORE THAN 6 MONTHS.

The effect of NICORETTE chewing pieces may be reduced by many foods or drinks such as coffee, juices, wine or soft drinks. Do not eat or drink for 15 minutes before or during use of NICORETTE chewing pieces.

SOME WAYS TO STOP YOUR USE OF NICORETTE CHEWING PIECES

(This is referred to as "weaning" from NICORETTE chewing pieces.)

As your urge to smoke fades, gradually use fewer pieces of NICORETTE. This may be possible in 2 to 3 months.

There are many possible ways for you to reduce your dose of NICORETTE. Below are some plans. Choose the plan or combinations of plans that works best for you.

As you reduce your use of NICORETTE chewing pieces, you should continue proper chewing procedures. See "HOW TO USE NICORETTE CHEWING PIECES" Steps 1 through 9.

* Every 4 to 7 days, reduce by 1 or more the number of pieces you use each day.

  For example: If you are using 12 pieces of NICORETTE a day, begin to use 11 pieces a day. Four to 7 days later, begin to use 10 pieces a day,. and so on.

* Use some pieces of NICORETTE for only 10 to 15 minutes instead of 30 minutes before throwing the gum away. Maintain the shorter time for each piece and also begin to gradually reduce the number of pieces used (see above example).

* You may want to chew each piece for longer than 30 minutes and reduce the number of pieces used each day.

* Use some sugarless gum in place of NICORETTE chewing pieces. Increase the number of sugarless gum pieces every 4 to 7 days.

  For example: If you are using 12 pieces of NICORETTE a day, begin to use 11 pieces of NICORETTE and 1 piece of sugarless gum.

  Four to 7 days later, use 10 pieces of NICORETTE and 2 pieces of sugarless gum.

  Keep using 1 more piece of sugarless gum and 1 less piece of NICORETTE every 4 to 7 days.

STOP USING NICORETTE WHEN YOU ARE SATISFIED WITH ONE OR TWO PIECES A DAY — UNLESS YOUR DOCTOR TELLS YOU OTHERWISE.

IF YOU HAVE TROUBLE IN REDUCING YOUR USE OF NICORETTE, CALL YOUR DOCTOR.

CARRY NICORETTE WITH YOU AT ALL TIMES IN CASE YOU FEEL THE URGE TO SMOKE AGAIN. ONE CIGARETTE IS ENOUGH TO START YOUR SMOKING HABIT AGAIN.

PRECAUTIONS

Ask your doctor about possible problems with NICORETTE chewing pieces. Be sure to tell your doctor if you have had any of the following:

* a recent heart attack (myocardial infarction)
* irregular heart beat (arrhythmia)
* severe or worsening heart pain (angina pectoris)
* temporomandibular joint disease (TMJ)
* allergies to drugs
* very high blood pressure
* stomach ulcers
* overactive thyroid
* diabetes requiring insulin
* kidney or liver disease
* mouth or throat inflammation
* heartburn (esophagitis)

If You Are Taking Medicines

The use of NICORETTE chewing pieces, together with stopping smoking, may change the effects of other medicines. It is important to tell your doctor about all the medicines you are taking.

What to Watch For (Adverse Effects)

Some people find it hard to stop using NICORETTE chewing pieces. This may occur for people who have depended on the nicotine in cigarettes. They may transfer that dependence to the nicotine in NICORETTE chewing pieces.

* Do not chew NICORETTE too fast or too hard. Doing this may cause the same effects as inhaling a cigarette for the first time or smoking too fast.

  Some of these effects are: light-headedness, nausea, vomiting, throat and mouth soreness, hiccups, and upset stomach.

* Some other effects which may occur, especially during the first few days of using NICORETTE chewing pieces, include: heart palpitations (flutterings), and more saliva in the mouth.

Most side effects can be controlled by chewing more slowly. Go over steps 3 through 7 under "HOW TO USE NICORETTE CHEWING PIECES."

If you swallow a piece of NICORETTE, you probably will have *no* side effects.

There are other side effects with the use of NICORETTE chewing pieces which have been reported. Your doctor can answer questions you may have about side effects. Report any problems to your doctor.

OVERDOSE

You should not smoke while using NICORETTE chewing pieces. It is possible to get too much nicotine, especially if you use NICORETTE chewing pieces and smoke at the same time.

Overdose may also occur if you chew many pieces of NICORETTE at one time or if you chew many pieces one right after another.

Signs of an overdose would include bad headaches, dizziness, upset stomach, drooling, vomiting, diarrhea, cold sweat, blurred vision, difficulty with hearing, mental confusion, and weakness. An overdose might cause you to faint.

What to Do When Problems Occur

IF YOU NOTICE ANY WORRISOME SYMPTOMS OR PROBLEMS, STOP USING NICORETTE CHEWING PIECES AND CALL YOUR DOCTOR AT ONCE.

OTHER INFORMATION

When you chew NICORETTE properly, nicotine is released slowly. It is absorbed through the lining of. your mouth. You may adjust the amount of nicotine you receive by changing how fast you chew NICORETTE and how much time you wait before another piece.

PLEASE NOTE

Like other gums, chewing NICORETTE may cause:
* injury to teeth
* injury to the lining of your mouth
* jaw ache
* belching when air is swallowed

Proper use of NICORETTE chewing pieces may reduce the chance that those effects may occur.

* Any gum may stick to your dentures, dental caps, or partial bridges. This may depend on the materials used in the dental work and other factors.

* NICORETTE chewing pieces are sugar free and have been made in such a way to reduce stickiness. If NICORETTE chewing pieces often stick to your dental work, there may be damage to the dental work. Stop using NICORETTE, and contact your doctor or dentist.

Storage Instructions

Store NICORETTE chewing pieces at room temperature, below 86°F (30°C). Remember, the inside of your car can reach temperatures much higher than this in the summer. Protect NICORETTE chewing pieces from light.

TO REMOVE GUM

Tear off single unit.

Peel off backing. Start at corner with loose edge.

Push gum through foil.

Product Information as of November 1992
J172N

NICODERM®
(nicotine transdermal system)

Systemic delivery of 21, 14, or 7 mg/day over 24 hours

DESCRIPTION
Nicoderm is a transdermal system that provides systemic delivery of nicotine for 24 hours following its application to intact skin.

Nicotine is a tertiary amine composed of a pyridine and a pyrrolidine ring. It is a colorless to pale yellow, freely water-soluble, strongly alkaline, oily, volatile, hygroscopic liquid obtained from the tobacco plant. Nicotine has a characteristic pungent odor and turns brown on exposure to air or light. Of its two stereoisomers, S(-)-nicotine is the more active and is the more prevalent form in tobacco. The free alkaloid is absorbed rapidly through the skin and respiratory tract.

Chemical Name: S-3-(1-methyl-2-pyrrolidinyl) pyridine
Molecular Formula: $C_{10}H_{14}N_2$
Molecular Weight: 162.23
Ionization Constants: $pK_a1 = 7.84$, $pK_a2 = 3.04$
Octanol-Water Partition Coefficient: 15:1 at pH 7

The Nicoderm system is a multilayered rectangular film containing nicotine as the active agent. For the three doses the composition per unit area is identical. Proceeding from the visible surface toward the surface attached to the skin are (1) an occlusive backing (polyethylene/aluminum/polyester/ethylene-vinyl acetate copolymer); (2) a drug reservoir containing nicotine (in an ethylene-vinyl acetate copolymer matrix); (3) a rate-controlling membrane (polyethylene); (4) a polyisobutylene adhesive; and (5) a protective liner that covers the adhesive layer and must be removed before application to the skin.

Occlusive Backing
Drug Reservoir
Rate-controlling Membrane
Contact Adhesive
Protective Liner

(not to scale)

Nicotine is the active ingredient; other components of the system are pharmacologically inactive.

The rate of delivery of nicotine to the patient from each system ($40 \mu g/cm^2$-h) is proportional to the surface area. About 73% of the total amount of nicotine remains in the system 24 hours after application. Nicoderm systems are labeled by the dose actually absorbed by the patient. The dose of nicotine absorbed from the Nicoderm system represents 68% of the amount released in 24 hours. The other 32% (eg, 9 mg/day for the 21 mg/day system) volatizes from the edge of the system.

Dose Absorbed in 24 Hours (mg/day)	System Area (cm^2)	Total Nicotine Content (mg)
21	22	114
14	15	78
7	7	36

CLINICAL PHARMACOLOGY
Pharmacologic Action
Nicotine, the chief alkaloid in tobacco products, binds stereoselectively to acetylcholine receptors at the autonomic ganglia, in the adrenal medulla, at neuromuscular junctions, and in the brain. Two types of central nervous system effects are believed to be the basis of nicotine's positively reinforcing properties. A stimulating effect, exerted mainly in the cortex via the locus ceruleus, produces increased alertness and cognitive performance. A "reward" effect via the "pleasure system" in the brain is exerted in the limbic system. At low doses the stimulant effects predominate, while at high doses the reward effects predominate. Intermittent intravenous

135

administration of nicotine activates neurohormonal pathways, releasing acetylcholine, norepinephrine, dopamine, serotonin, vasopressin, beta-endorphin, growth hormone, and ACTH.

Pharmacodynamics
The cardiovascular effects of nicotine include peripheral vasoconstriction, tachycardia, and elevated blood pressure. Acute and chronic tolerance to nicotine develops from smoking tobacco or ingesting nicotine preparations. Acute tolerance (a reduction in response for a given dose) develops rapidly (less than 1 hour), but at distinct rates for different physiologic effects (skin temperature, heart rate, subjective effects). Withdrawal symptoms, such as cigarette craving, can be reduced in some individuals by plasma nicotine levels lower than those for smoking.

Withdrawal from nicotine in addicted individuals is characterized by craving, nervousness, restlessness, irritability, mood lability, anxiety, drowsiness, sleep disturbances, impaired concentration, increased appetite, minor somatic complaints (headache, myalgia, constipation, fatigue), and weight gain. Nicotine toxicity is characterized by nausea, abdominal pain, vomiting, diarrhea, diaphoresis, flushing, dizziness, disturbed hearing and vision, confusion, weakness, palpitations, altered respiration, and hypotension.

The cardiovascular effects of Nicoderm 21 mg/day used continuously for 24 hours and smoking every 30 minutes during waking hours for 5 days were compared. Both regimens elevated heart rate (about 10 beats/min) and blood pressure (about 5 mm Hg) compared with an abstinence period, and these increases were similar between treatments throughout the 24-hour period, including during sleep.

The circadian pattern and release of plasma cortisol following 5 days of treatment with Nicoderm 21 mg/day did not differ from that following 5 days of nicotine abstinence. Urinary excretion of norepinephrine, epinephrine, and dopamine was also similar for Nicoderm 21 mg/day and abstinence.

Pharmacokinetics
Following application of the Nicoderm system to the upper body or upper outer arm, approximately 68% of the nicotine released from the system enters the systemic circulation (eg, 21 mg/day for the highest dose of Nicoderm). The remainder of the nicotine released from the system is lost via evaporation from the edge. All Nicoderm systems are labeled by the actual amount of nicotine absorbed by the patient.

The volume of distribution following IV administration of nicotine is approximately 2 to 3 L/kg, and the half-life of nicotine ranges from 1 to 2 hours. The major eliminating organ is the liver, and average plasma clearance is about 1.2 L/min; the kidney and lung also metabolize nicotine. There is no significant skin metabolism of nicotine. More than 20 metabolites of nicotine have been identified, all of which are believed to be less active than the parent compound. The primary metabolite of nicotine in plasma, cotinine, has a half-life of 15 to 20 hours and concentrations that exceed nicotine by 10-fold.

Plasma protein binding of nicotine is <5%. Therefore, changes in nicotine binding from use of concomitant drugs or alterations of plasma proteins by disease states would not be expected to have significant consequences.

The primary urinary metabolites are cotinine (15% of the dose) and trans-3-hydroxycotinine (45% of the dose). About 10% of nicotine is excreted unchanged in the urine. As much as 30% may be excreted in the urine with high urine flow rates and urine acidification below pH 5.

After Nicoderm application, plasma concentrations rise rapidly, plateau within 2 to 4 hours, and then slowly decline until the system is removed; after which they decline more rapidly.

The pharmacokinetic model that best fits the plasma nicotine concentrations from Nicoderm systems is an open, two-compartment disposition model with a skin depot through which nicotine enters the central circulation compartment. Nicotine in the adhesive layer is absorbed into and then through the skin, causing the initial rapid rise in plasma concentrations. The nicotine from the reservoir is released slowly through the membrane with a release rate constant approximately 20 times smaller than the skin absorption rate constant, as demonstrated *in vitro* in cadaver skin flux studies and verified by pharmacokinetic trials. Therefore, the slow decline of plasma nicotine concentrations during 4 to 24 hours (see Figure) is determined primarily by the release of nicotine from the system.

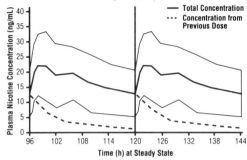

Steady-State Plasma Nicotine Concentrations for Two Consecutive Applications of Nicoderm 21 mg/day (Mean ±2 SD)

— Total Concentration
--- Concentration from Previous Dose

Following the second daily Nicoderm system application, steady-state plasma nicotine concentrations are achieved and are on average 30% higher compared with single-dose applications. Plasma nicotine concentrations are proportional to dose (ie, linear kinetics are observed) for the three dosages of Nicoderm systems. Nicotine kinetics are similar for all sites of application on the upper body and upper outer arm. Plasma nicotine concentrations from Nicoderm 21 mg/day are the same as those from simultaneous use of Nicoderm 14 mg/day and 7 mg/day.

Following removal of the Nicoderm system, plasma nicotine concentrations decline in an exponential fashion with an apparent mean half-life of 3 to 4 hours (see dotted line in Figure) compared with 1 to 2 hours for IV administration, due to continued absorption from the skin depot. Most nonsmoking patients will have nondetectable nicotine concentrations in 10 to 12 hours.

Steady-State Nicotine Pharmacokinetic Parameters for Nicoderm Systems (Mean, SD, and Range)

	Dose Absorbed (mg/day)								
	21			**14**			**7**		
	Mean	SD	Range	Mean	SD	Range	Mean	SD	Range
C_{max} ng/mL	23	5	13-32	17	3	10-24	8	2	5-12
C_{avg} ng/mL	17	4	10-26	12	3	8-17	6	1	4-10
C_{min} ng/mL	11	3	6-17	7	2	4-11	4	1	3-6
T_{max} h	4	3	1-10	4	3	1-10	4	4	1-18

C_{max} : maximum observed plasma concentration
C_{avg} : average plasma concentration
C_{min} : minimum observed plasma concentration
T_{max} : time of maximum plasma concentration

Half-hourly smoking of cigarettes produces average plasma nicotine concentrations of approximately 44 ng/mL. In comparison, average plasma nicotine concentrations from Nicoderm 21 mg/day are about 17 ng/mL.

There are no differences in nicotine kinetics between men and women using Nicoderm systems. Linear regression of both AUC and C_{max} vs total body weight shows the expected inverse relationship. Obese men using Nicoderm systems had significantly lower AUC and C_{max} values than normal weight men. Men and women having low body weight are expected to have higher AUC and C_{max} values.

137

CLINICAL STUDIES

The efficacy of Nicoderm systems as an aid to smoking cessation was demonstrated in two placebo-controlled, double-blind trials of otherwise healthy patients (n=756) smoking at least one pack of cigarettes per day. The trials consisted of 6 weeks of active treatment, 6 weeks of weaning off Nicoderm systems, and 12 weeks of follow-up on no medication. Quitting was defined as total abstinence from smoking (as determined by patient diary and verified by expired carbon monoxide). The "quit rates" are the proportion of patients enrolled who abstained after week 2.

The two trials in otherwise healthy smokers showed that all Nicoderm doses were more effective than placebo, and that treatment with Nicoderm 21 mg/day for 6 weeks provided significantly higher quit rates than the 14 mg/day and placebo treatments at 6 weeks. Data from these two studies are combined in the Quit Rate table. Quit rates were still significantly different after an additional 6-week weaning period and at follow-up 3 months later. All patients were given weekly behavioral supportive care. As shown in the following table, the quit rates on each treatment varied 2- to 3-fold among clinics at 6 weeks.

Quit Rates After Week 2 According to Starting Dose
(N=756 smokers in 9 clinics)

Nicoderm Delivery Rate (mg/day)	Number of Patients	After 6 Weeks Range*	After Weaning Range*	At 6 Months Range*
21	249	32-92%	18-63%	3-50%
14	254	30-61%	15-52%	0-48%
Placebo	253	15-46%	0-38%	0-35%

*Range for 9 centers, number of patients per treatment ranged from 23-34

In a study of smokers with coronary artery disease, 77 patients treated with Nicoderm systems (75% on 14 mg/day and 25% on 21 mg/day) had higher quit rates than 78 placebo-treated patients at the end of the 8-week study period (5 weeks of active treatment and 3 weeks of weaning). Nicoderm systems did not affect angina frequency or the appearance of arrhythmias on Holter monitoring in these patients. Symptoms presumed related to nicotine withdrawal and the stress of smoking cessation caused more patients to terminate the study than symptoms thought to be related to nicotine substitution. Seven patients on placebo and one on Nicoderm 14 mg/day dropped out for symptoms probably related to nicotine withdrawal (7 of these 8 patients experienced cardiovascular symptoms), while only two patients dropped out for nicotine-related symptoms (one patient with severe nausea on Nicoderm 14 mg/day and one with nausea and palpitations on Nicoderm 21 mg/day).

Patients who used Nicoderm systems in clinical trials had a significant reduction in craving for cigarettes, a major nicotine withdrawal symptom, compared with placebo-treated patients (see Figure). Reduction in craving, as with quit rate, is quite variable. This variability is presumed to be due to inherent differences in patient populations (eg, patient motivation, concomitant illnesses, number of cigarettes smoked per day, number of years smoking, exposure to other smokers, socioeconomic status) as well as differences among the clinics.

Severity of Craving by Treatment From Clinical Trials (N=877)

138

Patients using Nicoderm systems dropped out of the trials less frequently than patients receiving placebo. Quit rates for the 56 patients over age 60 were comparable to the quit rates for the 821 patients aged 60 and under.

Individualization of Dosage
It is important to make sure that patients read the instructions made available to them and have their questions answered. They should clearly understand the directions for applying and disposing of Nicoderm systems. They should be instructed to stop smoking completely when the first system is applied.

The success or failure of smoking cessation depends heavily on the quality, intensity, and frequency of supportive care. Patients are more likely to quit smoking if they are seen frequently and participate in formal smoking-cessation programs.

The goal of Nicoderm therapy is complete abstinence. Significant health benefits have not been demonstrated for reduction of smoking. If a patient is unable to stop smoking by the fourth week of therapy, treatment should probably be discontinued. Patients who have not stopped smoking after 4 weeks of Nicoderm therapy are unlikely to quit on that attempt.

Patients who fail to quit on any attempt may benefit from interventions to improve their chances for success on subsequent attempts. These patients should be counselled to determine why they failed and then probably be given a "therapy holiday" before the next attempt. A new quit attempt should be encouraged when the factors that contributed to failure can be eliminated or reduced, and conditions are more favorable.

Based on the clinical trials, a reasonable approach to assisting patients in their attempt to quit smoking is to assign their initial Nicoderm treatment using the recommended dosing schedule (see Dosing Schedule below). The need for dose adjustment should be assessed during the first 2 weeks. Patients should continue the dose selected with counselling and support over the following month. Those who have successfully stopped smoking during that time should be supported during 4 to 8 weeks of weaning, after which treatment should be terminated.

Therapy generally should begin with the Nicoderm 21 mg/day (see Dosing Schedule below) except if the patient is small (less than 100 pounds), is a light smoker (less than $\frac{1}{2}$ pack of cigarettes per day), or has cardiovascular disease.

Dosing Schedule

	Otherwise Healthy Patients	Other* Patients
Initial/Starting Dose	21 mg/day	14 mg/day
Duration of Treatment	4-8 weeks	4-8 weeks
First Weaning Dose	14 mg/day	7 mg/day
Duration of Treatment	2-4 weeks	2-4 weeks
Second Weaning Dose	7 mg/day	
Duration of Treatment	2-4 weeks	

* Small patient (less than 100 pounds)
or light smoker (less than 10 cigarettes/day)
or patient with cardiovascular disease

The symptoms of nicotine withdrawal and excess overlap (see *Pharmacodynamics* and ADVERSE REACTIONS). Since patients using Nicoderm systems may also smoke intermittently, it may be difficult to determine if patients are experiencing nicotine withdrawal or nicotine excess.

The controlled clinical trials using Nicoderm therapy suggest that abnormal dreams and insomnia are more often symptoms of nicotine excess, while anxiety, somnolence, and depression are more often symptoms of nicotine withdrawal.

INDICATIONS AND USAGE
Nicoderm treatment is indicated as an aid to smoking cessation for the relief of nicotine withdrawal symptoms. Nicoderm treatment should be used as part of a comprehensive behavioral smoking-cessation program.

139

The use of Nicoderm systems for longer than 3 months has not been studied.

CONTRAINDICATIONS

Use of Nicoderm systems is contraindicated in patients with hypersensitivity or allergy to nicotine or to any of the components of the therapeutic system.

WARNINGS

Nicotine from any source can be toxic and addictive. Smoking causes lung cancer, heart disease, and emphysema and may adversely affect the fetus and the pregnant woman. For any smoker, with or without concomitant disease or pregnancy, the risk of nicotine replacement in a smoking-cessation program should be weighed against the hazard of continued smoking while using Nicoderm systems and the likelihood of achieving cessation of smoking without nicotine replacement.

Pregnancy Warning

Tobacco smoke, which has been shown to be harmful to the fetus, contains nicotine, hydrogen cyanide, and carbon monoxide. Nicotine has been shown in animal studies to cause fetal harm. It is therefore presumed that Nicoderm systems can cause fetal harm when administered to a pregnant woman. The effect of nicotine delivery by Nicoderm systems has not been examined in pregnancy (see PRECAUTIONS).

Therefore pregnant smokers should be encouraged to attempt cessation using educational and behavioral interventions before using pharmacological approaches. If Nicoderm systems are used during pregnancy, or if the patient becomes pregnant while using Nicoderm systems, the patient should be apprised of the potential hazard to the fetus.

Safety Note Concerning Children

The amounts of nicotine that are tolerated by adult smokers can produce symptoms of poisoning and could prove fatal if the Nicoderm system is applied or ingested by children or pets. Used 21 mg/day systems contain about 73% (83 mg) of their initial drug content. Therefore, patients should be cautioned to keep both the used and unused Nicoderm systems out of the reach of children and pets.

PRECAUTIONS

The patient should be urged to stop smoking completely when initiating Nicoderm therapy (see DOSAGE AND ADMINISTRATION). Patients should be informed that if they continue to smoke while using Nicoderm systems, they may experience adverse effects due to peak nicotine levels higher than those experienced from smoking alone. If there is a clinically significant increase in cardiovascular or other effects attributable to nicotine, the Nicoderm dose should be reduced or Nicoderm treatment discontinued (see WARNINGS). Physicians should anticipate that concomitant medications may need dosage adjustment (see *Drug Interactions*).

The use of Nicoderm systems beyond 3 months by patients who stop smoking should be discouraged, because the chronic consumption of nicotine by any route can be harmful and addicting.

Allergic Reactions

In a 6-week, open-label, dermal irritation and sensitization study of Nicoderm systems, 7 of 230 patients exhibited definite erythema at 24 hours after application. Upon rechallenge, 4 patients exhibited mild to moderate contact allergy. Patients with contact sensitization should be cautioned that a serious reaction could occur from exposure to other nicotine-containing products or smoking. In the efficacy trials, erythema following system removal was typically seen in about 14% of patients, some edema in 3%, and dropouts due to skin reactions occurred in 2% of patients.

Patients should be instructed to promptly discontinue the use of Nicoderm systems and contact their physicians, if they experience severe or persistent local skin reactions (eg, severe erythema, pruritus, or edema) at the site of application or a generalized skin reaction (eg, urticaria, hives, or generalized rash).

Patients using Nicoderm therapy concurrently with other transdermal products may exhibit local reactions at both application sites. Reactions were seen in 2 of 7 patients using concomitant Estraderm® (estradiol transdermal system) in clinical trials. In such patients, use of one or both systems may have to be discontinued.

140

Skin Disease
Nicoderm systems are usually well tolerated by patients with normal skin, but may be irritating for patients with some skin disorders (atopic or eczematous dermatitis).

Cardiovascular or Peripheral Vascular Diseases
The risks of nicotine replacement in patients with certain cardiovascular and peripheral vascular diseases should be weighed against the benefits of including nicotine replacement in a smoking-cessation program for them. Specifically, patients with coronary heart disease (history of myocardial infarction and/or angina pectoris), serious cardiac arrhythmias, or vasospastic diseases (Buerger's disease, Prinzmetal's variant angina) should be carefully screened and evaluated before nicotine replacement is prescribed.

Tachycardia occurring in association with the use of Nicoderm therapy was reported occasionally. If serious cardiovascular symptoms occur with the use of Nicoderm therapy, it should be discontinued.

Nicoderm therapy was as well tolerated as placebo in a controlled trial in patients with coronary artery disease (see CLINICAL STUDIES). One patient on Nicoderm 21 mg/day, two on Nicoderm 14 mg/day, and eight on placebo discontinued treatment due to adverse events.

Nicoderm therapy did not affect angina frequency or the appearance of arrhythmias on Holter monitoring in these patients.

Nicoderm therapy generally should not be used in patients during the immediate post-myocardial infarction period, patients with serious arrhythmias, and patients with severe or worsening angina pectoris.

Renal or Hepatic Insufficiency
The pharmacokinetics of nicotine have not been studied in the elderly or in patients with renal or hepatic impairment. However, given that nicotine is extensively metabolized and that its total system clearance is dependent on liver blood flow, some influence of hepatic impairment on drug kinetics (reduced clearance) should be anticipated. Only severe renal impairment would be expected to affect the clearance of nicotine or its metabolites from the circulation (see *Pharmacokinetics*).

Endocrine Diseases
Nicoderm therapy should be used with caution in patients with hyperthyroidism, pheochromocytoma, or insulin-dependent diabetes, since nicotine causes the release of catecholamines by the adrenal medulla.

Peptic Ulcer Disease
Nicotine delays healing in peptic ulcer disease; therefore, Nicoderm therapy should be used with caution in patients with active peptic ulcers and only when the benefits of including nicotine replacement in a smoking-cessation program outweigh the risks.

Accelerated Hypertension
Nicotine therapy constitutes a risk factor for development of malignant hypertension in patients with accelerated hypertension; therefore, Nicoderm therapy should be used with caution in these patients and only when the benefits of including nicotine replacement in a smoking-cessation program outweigh the risks.

Information for Patient
A patient instruction booklet is included in the package of Nicoderm systems dispensed to the patient. The instruction sheet contains important information and instructions on how to properly use and dispose of Nicoderm systems. Patients should be encouraged to ask questions of the physician and pharmacist.

Patients must be advised to keep both used and unused systems out of the reach of children and pets.

Drug Interactions
Smoking cessation, with or without nicotine replacement, may alter the pharmacokinetics of certain concomitant medications.

May Require a Decrease in Dose at Cessation of Smoking	Possible Mechanism
acetaminophen, caffeine, imipramine, oxazepam, pentazocine, propranolol, theophylline	Deinduction of hepatic enzymes on smoking cessation.
insulin	Increase in subcutaneous insulin absorption with smoking cessation.
adrenergic antagonists (eg, prazosin, labetalol)	Decrease in circulating catecholamines with smoking cessation.

May Require an Increase in Dose at Cessation of Smoking	Possible Mechanism
adrenergic agonists (eg, isoproterenol, phenylephrine)	Decrease in circulating catecholamines with smoking cessation.

Carcinogenesis, Mutagenesis, Impairment of Fertility
Nicotine itself does not appear to be a carcinogen in laboratory animals. However, nicotine and its metabolites increased the incidences of tumors in the cheek pouches of hamsters and forestomach of F344 rats, respectively, when given in combination with tumor initiators. One study, which could not be replicated, suggested that cotinine, the primary metabolite of nicotine, may cause lymphoreticular sarcoma in the large intestine in rats.

Nicotine and cotinine were not mutagenic in the Ames *Salmonella* test. Nicotine induced repairable DNA damage in an *E. coli* test system. Nicotine was shown to be genotoxic in a test system using Chinese hamster ovary cells. In rats and rabbits, implantation can be delayed or inhibited by a reduction in DNA synthesis that appears to be caused by nicotine. Studies have shown a decrease in litter size in rats treated with nicotine during gestation.

Pregnancy
Pregnancy Category D (see WARNINGS).

The harmful effects of cigarette smoking on maternal and fetal health are clearly established. These include low birth weight, increased risk of spontaneous abortion, and increased perinatal mortality. The specific effects of Nicoderm therapy on fetal development are unknown. Therefore pregnant smokers should be encouraged to attempt cessation using educational and behavioral interventions before using pharmacological approaches.

Spontaneous abortion during nicotine replacement therapy has been reported; as with smoking, nicotine as a contributing factor cannot be excluded.

Nicoderm therapy should be used during pregnancy only if the likelihood of smoking cessation justifies the potential risk of use of nicotine replacement by the patient who may continue to smoke.

Teratogenicity
Animal Studies: Nicotine was shown to produce skeletal abnormalities in the offspring of mice when given doses toxic to the dams (25 mg/kg IP or SC).

Human Studies: Nicotine teratogenicity has not been studied in humans except as a component of cigarette smoke (each cigarette smoked delivers about 1 mg of nicotine). It has not been possible to conclude whether cigarette smoking is teratogenic to humans.

Other Effects
Animal Studies: A nicotine bolus (up to 2 mg/kg) to pregnant rhesus monkeys caused acidosis, hypercarbia, and hypotension (fetal and maternal concentrations were about 20 times those achieved after smoking 1 cigarette in 5 minutes). Fetal breathing movements were reduced in the fetal lamb after intravenous injection of 0.25 mg/kg nicotine to the ewe (equivalent to smoking 1 cigarette every 20 seconds for 5 minutes).

142

Uterine blood flow was reduced about 30% after infusion of 0.1 mg/kg/min nicotine for 20 minutes to pregnant rhesus monkeys (equivalent to smoking about 6 cigarettes every minute for 20 minutes).

Human Experience: Cigarette smoking during pregnancy is associated with an increased risk of spontaneous abortion, low birth weight infants, and perinatal mortality. Nicotine and carbon monoxide are considered the most likely mediators of these outcomes. The effect of cigarette smoking on fetal cardiovascular parameters has been studied near term. Cigarettes increased fetal aortic blood flow and heart rate and decreased uterine blood flow and fetal breathing movements. Nicoderm therapy has not been studied in pregnant humans.

Labor and Delivery
The Nicoderm system is not recommended to be left on during labor and delivery. The effects of nicotine on a mother or the fetus during labor are unknown.

Use in Nursing Mothers
Caution should be exercised when Nicoderm therapy is administered to nursing women. The safety of Nicoderm therapy in nursing infants has not been examined. Nicotine passes freely into breast milk; the milk to plasma ratio averages 2.9. Nicotine is absorbed orally. An infant has the ability to clear nicotine by hepatic first-pass clearance; however, the efficiency of removal is probably lowest at birth. The nicotine concentrations in milk can be expected to be lower with Nicoderm therapy, when used as directed, than with cigarette smoking, as maternal plasma nicotine concentrations are generally reduced with nicotine replacement. The risk of exposure of the infant to nicotine from Nicoderm therapy should be weighed against the risks associated with the infant's exposure to nicotine from continued smoking by the mother (passive smoke exposure and contamination of breast milk with other components of tobacco smoke) and from Nicoderm therapy alone or in combination with continued smoking.

Pediatric Use
Nicoderm therapy is not recommended for use in children, because the safety and effectiveness of Nicoderm therapy in children and adolescents who smoke have not been evaluated.

Geriatric Use
Fifty-six patients over the age of 60 participated in clinical trials of Nicoderm therapy. Nicoderm therapy appeared to be as effective in this age group as in younger smokers. However, asthenia, various body aches, and dizziness occurred slightly more often in patients over 60 years of age.

ADVERSE REACTIONS
Assessment of adverse events in the 1,131 patients who participated in controlled clinical trials is complicated by the occurrence of GI and CNS effects of nicotine withdrawal as well as nicotine excess. The actual incidences of both are confounded by concurrent smoking by many of the patients. When reporting adverse events during the trials, the investigators did not attempt to identify the cause of the symptom.

Topical Adverse Events
The most common adverse event associated with topical nicotine is a short-lived erythema, pruritus, and/or burning at the application site, which was seen at least once in 47% of patients on the Nicoderm system in the clinical trials. Local erythema after system removal was noted at least once in 14% of patients and local edema in 3%. Erythema generally resolved within 24 hours. Cutaneous hypersensitivity (contact sensitization) occurred in 2% of patients on Nicoderm systems (see PRECAUTIONS, *Allergic Reactions*).

Probably Causally Related

The following adverse events were reported more frequently in Nicoderm-treated patients than in placebo-treated patients or exhibited a dose response in clinical trials.

Digestive system — Diarrhea*, dyspepsia*
Mouth/Tooth disorders — Dry mouth+
Musculoskeletal system — Arthralgia+, myalgia*
Nervous system — Abnormal dreams*, insomnia (23%),
nervousness*
Skin and appendages — Sweating+

143

Frequencies for 21 mg/day system
* Reported in 3% to 9% of patients
+ Reported in 1% to 3 % of patients
Unmarked if reported in <1% of patients

Causal Relationship UNKNOWN
Adverse events reported in Nicoderm- and placebo-treated patients at about the same frequency in clinical trials are listed below. The clinical significance of the association between Nicoderm systems and these events is unknown, but they are reported as alerting information for the clinician.

Body as a whole — Asthenia*, back pain*, chest pain+, pain*
Digestive system — Abdominal pain+, constipation*, nausea*, vomiting+
Nervous system — Dizziness*, headache (29%), paresthesia+
Respiratory system — Cough increased*, pharyngitis*, sinusitis+
Skin and appendages — Rash*
Special senses — Taste perversion*
Urogenital system — Dysmenorrhea*

Frequencies for 21 mg/day systems
* Reported in 3% to 9% of patients
+ Reported in 1% to 3 % of patients
Unmarked if reported in <1% of patients

DRUG ABUSE AND DEPENDENCE
Nicoderm therapy is likely to have a low abuse potential based on differences between it and cigarettes in four characteristics commonly considered important in contributing to abuse: much slower absorption, much smaller fluctuations in blood levels, lower blood levels of nicotine, and less frequent use (ie, once daily).

Dependence on nicotine polacrilex chewing gum replacement therapy has been reported. Such dependence might also occur from transference to Nicoderm systems of tobacco-based nicotine dependence. The use of the system beyond 3 months has not been evaluated and should be discouraged.

To minimize the risk of dependence, patients should be encouraged to withdraw gradually from Nicoderm treatment after 4 to 8 weeks of use. Recommended dose reduction is to progressively decrease the dose every 2 to 4 weeks (see DOSAGE AND ADMINISTRATION).

OVERDOSAGE
The effects of applying several Nicoderm systems simultaneously or swallowing Nicoderm systems are unknown (see WARNINGS, *Safety Note Concerning Children*).

The oral LD_{50} for nicotine in rodents varies with species but is in excess of 24 mg/kg; death is due to respiratory paralysis. The oral minimum lethal dose of nicotine in dogs is greater than 5 mg/kg. The oral minimum acute lethal dose for nicotine in human adults is reported to be 40 to 60 mg (<1 mg/kg).

Three dogs, each weighing 11 kg, were fed two damaged Nicoderm 14 mg/day systems. Nicotine plasma concentrations of 32 to 79 ng/mL were observed. No ill effects were apparent.

Signs and symptoms of an overdose from a Nicoderm system would be expected to be the same as those of acute nicotine poisoning, including pallor, cold sweat, nausea, salivation, vomiting, abdominal pain, diarrhea, headache, dizziness, disturbed hearing and vision, tremor, mental confusion, and weakness. Prostration, hypotension, and respiratory failure may ensue with large overdoses. Lethal doses produce convulsions quickly, and death follows as a result of peripheral or central respiratory paralysis or, less frequently, cardiac failure.

Overdose From Topical Exposure
The Nicoderm system should be removed immediately if the patient shows signs of overdosage, and the patient should seek immediate medical care. The skin surface may be flushed with water and dried. No soap should be used, since it may increase nicotine absorption. Nicotine will continue to be delivered into the bloodstream for several hours (see *Pharmacokinetics*) after removal of the system because of a depot of nicotine in the skin.

Overdose From Ingestion

Persons ingesting Nicoderm systems should be referred to a health care facility for management. Due to the possibility of nicotine-induced seizures, activated charcoal should be administered. In unconscious patients with a secure airway, instill activated charcoal via a nasogastric tube. A saline cathartic or sorbitol added to the first dose of activated charcoal may speed gastrointestinal passage of the system. Repeated doses of activated charcoal should be administered as long as the system remains in the gastrointestinal tract since it will continue to release nicotine for many hours.

Management of Nicotine Poisoning

Other supportive measures include diazepam or barbiturates for seizures, atropine for excessive bronchial secretions or diarrhea, respiratory support for respiratory failure, and vigorous fluid support for hypotension and cardiovascular collapse.

DOSAGE AND ADMINISTRATION

Patients must desire to stop smoking and should be instructed to *stop smoking immediately* as they begin using Nicoderm therapy. The patient should read the patient instruction booklet on Nicoderm therapy and be encouraged to ask any questions. Treatment should be initiated with Nicoderm 21 mg/day or 14 mg/day systems (see *Individualization of Dosage*).

Once the appropriate dosage is selected the patient should begin 4 to 6 weeks of therapy at that dosage. The patient should stop smoking cigarettes completely during this period. If the patient is unable to stop cigarette smoking within 4 weeks, Nicoderm therapy probably should be stopped, since few additional patients in clinical trials were able to quit after this time.

Recommended Dosing Schedule for Healthy Patients[a]
(See *Individualization of Dosage*)

Dose	Duration
Nicoderm 21 mg/day	First 6 Weeks
Nicoderm 14 mg/day	Next 2 Weeks[b]
Nicoderm 7 mg/day	Last 2 Weeks[c]

[a] Start with Nicoderm 14 mg/day for 6 weeks for patients who:
- have cardiovascular disease
- weigh less than 100 pounds
- smoke less than 1/2 a pack of cigarettes/day

Decrease dose to Nicoderm 7 mg/day for the final 2-4 weeks.

[b] Patients who have successfully abstained from smoking should have their dose of Nicoderm reduced after each 2-4 weeks of treatment until the 7 mg/day dose has been used for 2-4 weeks (see *Individualization of Dosage*).

[c] The entire course of nicotine substitution and gradual withdrawal should take 8-12 weeks, depending on the size of the initial dose. The use of Nicoderm systems beyond 3 months has not been studied.

The Nicoderm system should be applied promptly upon its removal from the protective pouch to prevent evaporative loss of nicotine from the system. Nicoderm systems should be used only when the pouch is intact to assure that the product has not been tampered with.

Nicoderm systems should be applied only once a day to a non-hairy, clean, dry skin site on the upper body or upper outer arm. After 24 hours, the used Nicoderm system should be removed and a new system applied to an alternate skin site. Skin sites should not be reused for at least a week. Patients should be cautioned not to continue to use the same system for more than 24 hours.

SAFETY AND HANDLING

The Nicoderm system can be a dermal irritant and can cause contact sensitization. Patients should be instructed in the proper use of Nicoderm systems by using demonstration systems. Although exposure of health care workers to nicotine from Nicoderm systems should be minimal, care should be taken to avoid unnecessary contact with active systems. If you do handle active systems, wash with water alone, since soap may increase nicotine absorption. Do not touch your eyes.

Disposal
When the used system is removed from the skin, it should be folded over and placed in the protective pouch that contained the new system. The used system should be immediately disposed of in such a way to prevent its access by children or pets. See patient information for further directions on handling and disposal.

How Supplied
See DESCRIPTION for total nicotine content per unit.

NDC 0088-0050-61
     Nicoderm 21 mg/day, 14 systems per box

NDC 0088-0051-61
     Nicoderm 14 mg/day, 14 systems per box

NDC 0088-0052-61
     Nicoderm 7 mg/day, 14 systems per box

How to Store
Do not store above 86°F (30°C) because Nicoderm systems are sensitive to heat. A slight discoloration of the system is not significant.

Do not store unpouched. Once removed from the protective pouch, Nicoderm systems should be applied promptly, since nicotine is volatile and the systems may lose strength.

CAUTION: Federal law prohibits dispensing without prescription.

Manufactured by
ALZA Corporation
Palo Alto, CA 94304 for
Marion Merrell Dow Inc.
Kansas City, MO 64114

Product Information as of January, 1992   J208C

NOTES

NOTES